CAPITAL STRUCTURING

CAPITAL STRUCTURING

Brian Coyle

CIB PUBLISHING

FINANCIAL
EDUCATION

CIB Publishing
c/o The Chartered Institute of Bankers
Emmanuel House
4-9 Burgate Lane
Canterbury
Kent
CT1 2XJ
United Kingdom

Telephone: 01227 762600

CIB Publishing publications are published by The Chartered Institute of Bankers, a non-profit making registered educational charity.

The Chartered Institute of Bankers believes that the sources of information upon which the book is based are reliable and has made every effort to ensure the complete accuracy of the text. However, neither CIB, the author nor any contributor can accept any legal responsibility whatsoever for consequences that may arise from errors or omissions or any opinion or advice given.

Typeset by The Foundry
Printed by WBC Book Manufacturers, Bridgend

© Chartered Institute of Bankers 2000

ISBN 0-85297-459-0

Contents

1. Introduction to Capital Structuring   1

2. Quantifying the Need for External Funds   11

3. Funding Options   25

4. Equity   51

5. Debt   63

6. Hybrid Financial Instruments   81

7. Optimal Capital Structure   91

8. Debt Profile Management   103

9. Refinancing   119

Glossary   131

Index   136

Introduction to Capital Structuring

In one way or another, business activity must be financed. Without finance to support their fixed assets and working capital requirements, businesses could not exist. There are three primary sources of finance for companies:

- a cash surplus from operating activities
- new equity funding
- borrowing from bank and non-bank sources. Non-bank sources are mainly investors in the capital markets who subscribe for bonds and other securities issued by companies.

New equity funding always should be available, at a price, to companies that can provide a good economic argument for wanting to raise money.

For many companies, however, all-equity finance is an unsatisfactory capital structure. Debt, because it is not permanent and can be much cheaper to service, is often an important ingredient in the funding mix. Debt capital, however, is not always available. Lenders could refuse funds to companies when the perceived credit risk is too high.

By taking into account a company's particular circumstances, management should decide what is the most appropriate mix of internal and external funding, and of equity and debt, i.e. how the company should structure the necessary capital to finance its activities.

Objectives

A variety of factors or objectives in the management of capital structuring will be explored more fully in later chapters, but briefly they are:

- deciding the optimal capital structure for a company, over a short-term and long-term planning period
- ensuring that funds are always available to finance the company's growth and development
- minimizing the cost of capital
- deciding how much to borrow, who or where from, when, for how long, and in what currency
- ensuring that money will be available to meet loan repayment obligations, and that refinancing would be available if required
- monitoring exposures to interest rate risk and, where appropriate, taking measures to hedge the risk.

A further objective might be to provide the company with the financial resources to continue trading in the event of a recession or downturn in one or more of its business markets.

Companies often will expect their financial advisers and bankers to assist in these matters.

Benefits of Debt Capital

Debt capital is provided mainly by two types of lender or investor. These are banks (bank loans and facilities) and institutional investors (for example, pension funds, mutual funds and life assurance companies), who invest in debt securities, such as bonds and commercial paper.

Debt capital has two important benefits for a profitable company needing external finance to grow and develop:

- cost
- flexibility.

Debt capital is often a fairly low-cost source of finance. Interest on debt is sometimes an allowable charge for tax purposes, and in such cases the cost of debt capital for a profitable company is therefore its after-tax cost. For example, when the rate of taxation on corporate profits is 30%, the effective after-tax cost of a 10% loan is just 7% (10% x 70%).

Many companies are able to raise debt capital at an attractive rate of interest, although the cost of any particular debt varies with circumstances, e.g. the debt instrument, the borrower's creditworthiness, the term of the loan, etc.

Debt is rarely perpetual, and must be redeemed at some future time. This can be an advantage to companies that need external funds for a limited number of years. Debt capital can be borrowed and repaid to suit the expected cash flows of a company, giving the company greater flexibility to plan and control its capital structure.

Example
Beta, a public company, is planning a $100 million investment that is expected to earn annual profits of $50 million for three years. The company has a good credit rating, and could borrow for three years at 6% per annum or for five years at 6.20% per annum. Current interest rates are considered low; they are unlikely to fall much further and could rise within the next two to three years.

A decision has been made to undertake the investment, but the method of funding, either an issue of new equity stock, or a bond issue, has yet to be decided.

Analysis
A drawback to equity funding is the permanence and cost of the funds. Equity stocks, once issued, are not easily cancelled, and stockholders will expect a satisfactory return.

One advantage of debt capital, particularly when interest rates are low, is that any surplus profits above the cost of financing the loan can be paid out to existing stockholders. A second advantage is that the company is not committed to a permanent increase in its long-term capital funds, because eventually the debt will be repaid. A further aspect of the flexibility of debt funding is the term of borrowing. The company needs the funds for an investment lasting just three years. However, the company has the option of borrowing for a longer term, say five years, in the belief that debt is currently very cheap, and it would be profitable in the long term to borrow for five years rather than for three years, even though the interest rate would be 20 basis points higher.

Debt and Creditworthiness

The major drawback to debt capital is the risk of being unable to meet the loan repayment obligations in full and on schedule. Companies with a high proportion of debt in their capital structure are likely to be considered a high credit risk by would-be lenders and investors. When a borrower's credit rating (or perceived creditworthiness) is low, the cost of borrowing could be very high, and the benefits of debt capital therefore much lower.

Credit ratings affect the cost of new borrowing. Suppose, for example, that a large multinational company suffers a fall in the credit rating on a bond issue from A to A-. As a consequence, the cost of raising new debt capital will go up, say, by 20 basis points (0.20%). To borrow $100 million would then cost the company an extra $200,000 ($100 million x 0.20%) each year in higher interest costs.

The Origins of Debt Management

Debt management is concerned with planning and controlling the debt element of a company's funding mix.

For a small company, borrowing effectively is limited to a loan (or facility) from one or more banks. A larger company, in contrast, has a wider range of debt markets available to it. Large companies can borrow from banks, or tap domestic, foreign or international markets for bonds, medium-term notes, commercial paper and hybrid instruments, e.g. convertible bonds.

Evolution of Markets

The origin of today's debt markets can be traced back to the creation of the eurodollar in the 1940s when under the Marshall Plan for economic recovery in Europe dollars could not be repatriated to the US. Eurodollars are simply dollars deposited with a bank outside the US. From the 1950s, a pool of offshore dollars accumulated with banks outside the US.

Over a period of time, this created a substantial pool of dollar-denominated funds held offshore by non-US citizens. This made very little impact on the international markets until the early 1960s. At this stage, in order to protect its domestic borrowers, the US authorities put in place a new tax. This was the interest equalization tax.

Because the rate of interest in the US was substantially lower than in most European countries, it became more advantageous for foreign borrowers to issue bonds in the domestic US market than in their home markets. This was still the Bretton Woods era of fixed exchange rates. In order to restrict the availability of dollar liquidity to domestic borrowers, the new tax charged overseas borrowers with the difference between the cost of borrowing in US dollars and the cost of borrowing in the borrowers' domestic currency. This effectively put a stop to foreign borrowers' access to US dollar funding. However, a few far-sighted investment bankers recognized that there was a huge supply of US dollars held offshore. They reasoned that if these dollars were lent to overseas borrowers, using securities issued outside the US, then the tax could not be applied. This was the start of the Eurobond market, a market that now issues $400 billion-worth of securities annually.

The eurodollar originated to accommodate governments in the old eastern bloc and the middle east, organizations and individuals (expatriate workers, etc.) who wanted to:

- hold dollars, then the reserve currency of the world, because the dollar was perceived as the currency offering the best protection against value depreciation, but at the same time,
- wanted to avoid exchange controls, the political risk of having dollar deposits seized and the regulation of dollar deposits by the US government that would have applied to dollars deposited in the US.

The pool of dollars held with banks outside the US was aggressively managed, and eurodollar investments were moved regularly to obtain higher yields in the relatively unregulated environment. The volume of eurodollar lending and borrowing grew as a result of:

- the premium yields paid on eurodollar deposits compared with domestic dollar deposits in the US
- the evolution of multinational banks and corporates
- the high dollar earnings of the oil-producing countries in the aftermath of the 1970s oil crisis, and the reluctance of these producers to place the dollars with banks in the US
- the demand from borrowers for dollar-denominated loans as a low-cost and stable source of funds, compared to the cost of borrowing in local currencies.

Over time, other eurocurrencies emerged. It became possible to hold other major currencies offshore, i.e. with banks outside the country of origin of the currency (deutschemarks, French francs, sterling, yen, etc.). For example, Swiss francs held offshore are likely to be deposited with an overseas (non-Swiss) branch of a bank that also has a branch or branches inside Switzerland. The customer's account might be with the London branch of Credit Suisse, thus allowing the customer to operate the Swiss franc account without being subject to the constraints of the Swiss banking system. At the same time the customer would benefit from the perceived stability of the Swiss franc and the interest yield available to holders of Swiss francs. The growth in eurocurrency markets can be measured by the fact that in aggregate, eurocurrency funds are now in excess of $2,000 billion.

Eurobonds

The requirement for higher yields by owners of eurocurrency deposits led to the development of the eurobond market in the early 1960s. The market developed to bring together institutions wishing to borrow in dollars with investors wishing to hold offshore dollar assets, i.e. bonds. It was successful largely because it was unregulated and easily accessible.

Eurobonds are debt securities that are distributed internationally and subsequently traded by dealers in several international financial centers. They are therefore purchased largely by investors with eurocurrency deposits, who are looking for a good return on their investments.

The initial market was for eurodollar bond issues only. Eventually other segments of the eurobond market developed, dedicated to euro-deutschemark, euro-yen, euro-sterling, etc. The market grew rapidly, feeding off its own success. Eurobonds became easily tradable, with widespread marketing outlets among banks.

- Investors were able to receive interest paid gross without any deduction of withholding tax.
- As the eurobond market grew in size, a market infrastructure also developed, with a more efficient secondary market and specialized settlement systems (Euroclear and Cedel).

Several domestic capital markets also have grown in recent years, encouraged by the removal of restrictions and regulations. These markets, such as the US private placement market and the yen public and private markets, have become much more accessible to foreign as well as to domestic borrowers.

A capital market cannot develop unless the increase in borrowing demand is matched by an increased supply of investor funds. Investor demand for eurobonds and other bonds grew for a number of reasons.

- *Liquidity.* Bonds can be sold into the secondary bond market and the proceeds applied to unforeseen funding requirements as they occur. The major bond markets in Europe and the US are highly liquid with continuous two-way prices available at narrow bid-offer spreads, allowing bonds to be bought or sold quickly with a single telephone call.

The ability to buy and sell bonds readily enables investors to switch the funds into investments denominated in different currencies as they shift their view about future changes in exchange rates.

- *Yield.* Borrowers are often prepared to pay premium yields to investors in return for a specific facility, such as a eurobond issue with relaxed covenants.
- *Foreign exchange exposure hedging.* Foreign exchange risk can be hedged by issuing bonds in a currency in which a company also has commercial receipts. By matching debt payments with an income stream in the same currency, it is possible to remove the risk of rising borrowing costs due to adverse exchange-rate movements. This would occur if the currency of borrowing strengthened against the borrower's domestic currency.
- *Tax benefits.* In some cases there can be substantial tax benefits in holding securities offshore.

Funding and the Capital Markets

Decisions about raising capital are influenced by investors' attitudes that borrowers cannot ignore. For example, a company cannot easily raise funds by issuing sterling commercial paper or by issuing bonds in the US private placement market, if there is insufficient interest in these markets for the planned issue. Similarly, a company cannot obtain a ten-year bank loan if banks are reluctant to lend beyond five years.

Market conditions therefore will affect decisions on how to raise new funds – for example, whether to issue new stocks, bonds or hybrid instruments, in which market, for what term and in what currency. Market conditions will also affect the timing and the cost of new issues.

Quantifying the Need For External Funds

Unless a company is certain that it can rely entirely on internally generated funds to finance its activities, it will have to estimate what its external funding requirements will be. In the debt management process, there is a repetitive cycle of

- estimating total external funding requirements, and the variation in these requirements over time
- organizing the total external funding requirements into three broad categories: long-term, short-term and contingency funding
- planning how and when to obtain the required funds, e.g. by issuing new equity or by borrowing.

Making an estimate of funding requirements is therefore the first step in the process of raising new capital. On some occasions, the prospectus of a company includes cash flow/capital funding projections over several years.

Cash Flow Forecast

An estimate of external funding requirements can be obtained from a cash flow forecast. The forecast must be reliable otherwise funding decisions cannot be taken with confidence. Reliability depends on accuracy, both as to the amount and the timing of cash flows. In addition, sensitivity analysis is required to assess the effect on funding requirements of different assumptions.

- *Quantitative accuracy*. Forecasts of cash flows should be as close to the actual amounts as possible. If a company's financial planners have developed a track record of accurate quantitative forecasts, greater reliance can be placed on their new forecasts.

- *Timing accuracy.* There should be a precise forecast of the timing of cash flows. Again, a track record of accurate forecasts should create confidence in new forecasts.

Obviously, absolute accuracy is not possible, and funding decisions must allow for a margin of error.

Why is Timing Accuracy Important?

It is easy to overlook the need for accuracy in forecasting the timing of cash flows, but there can be serious risks or high extra costs implicit in an inaccurate timing estimate.

Example

A company anticipates a customer's progress payment of $10 million for a major contract. The customer disputes the quality of the work on the contract, and the company's forecast of receiving the money in June proves over-optimistic.

Analysis

If the company has relied on the progress payment from the customer to meet its funding requirements, and does not have arrangements for contingency funding it will have a cash shortfall of $10 million in June. It must try to make up the shortfall urgently, perhaps by borrowing at an unfavorable rate.

Items in a Cash Flow Forecast

The details of how to prepare a cash flow forecast are not covered in this book; forecasting techniques are more relevant to a book on cash management, such as *Series 3 – Cash Flow Management.* However, it is important to appreciate what a forecast should contain, and how it might best be structured for the purpose of short-term and long-term funding estimates.

There are a number of important items that should be included in a cash flow forecast:

- Cash flows from operating activities
- interest payments (and receipts)
- dividend payments (and receipts)
- payments of tax
- repayment of principal on loans
- capital expenditures.

Unless it is certain that external funds will be raised during the forecast period, estimates of new funding should be excluded from the forecast.

With fixed-rate borrowing, the amount and timing of repayments can be forecast exactly. With variable-rate borrowing, reasonable estimates of interest costs should be made (and the interest rate up to the next reset date will in any case be known, so that the short-term forecast of loan payments should be exact).

Some items of income or expenditure might be discretionary, and subject perhaps to future decisions by senior management. Examples are the cost of acquiring a new subsidiary, or the disposal of fixed assets, or a part of the company's business. Potential items of cash flow that would involve large amounts of money are usually excluded from the forecast. Should funds be needed for a discretionary project, a separate decision is taken on how to raise the finance.

Time Periods and Planning Horizon

A cash flow forecast should have an end date or planning horizon. Long-term forecasts will be less accurate than forecasts covering a shorter period. The most suitable planning horizon will depend on the company's circumstances, and the term over which it might borrow new funds.

A large company that borrows regularly for terms of five to ten years should prepare forecasts for at least a five-to-ten-year period. A small company relying entirely on operating cash flows and a bank overdraft will have a much shorter planning horizon, typically just 12 months to two years.

Cash flow forecasts should be divided into time periods. Dividing a forecast into periods of one day, one week, one month, one quarter, six months or one year should

- coincide as closely as possible with significant cash flow events, and
- reflect the required accuracy of the forecast.

A large company with a high volume of cash flows could have:

- a six-week forecast updated weekly, with the first two weeks analyzed into daily flows
- a 12-month rolling forecast analyzed month-by-month, with a new forecast produced monthly
- a five- or 10-year forecast analyzed year-by-year and compiled annually, with perhaps an update, i.e. a revised forecast, after six months.

Each forecast should have its specific uses, either for day-to-day cash management or for funding and debt-management decisions. This book is concerned primarily with longer-term cash forecasts because these are most relevant to debt management and capital structuring.

Example
A company has prepared a five-year cash forecast, divided into time periods of six months for the first two years and time periods of one year thereafter. It is assumed in the forecast that no external funds will be used. The forecasts are as follows:

	Year 1 1st 6 mths	Year 1 2nd 6 mths	Year 2 1st 6 mths	Year 2 2nd 6 mths	Year 3	Year 4	Year 5
	$000	$000	$000	$000	$000	$000	$000
Operational cash flows	+270	+240	+290	+250	+580	+600	+620
Investment income	+20	+20	+18	+16	+35	+35	+30
	+290	+260	+308	+266	+615	+635	+650
Loan and interest payments	-25	-25	-425	-10	-10	0	0
Dividend payments	-80	-84	-88	-90	-92		
Tax payments	-120	-20	-140	-21	-150	-155	-160
Capital expenditure	-125	-180	-150	-125	-250	-260	-270
	-350	-225	-799	-156	-498	-505	-522
Sale of division (to be decided)			+250				

The company currently has a cash surplus of $10,000.

Analysis

A simple cash forecast can be obtained from this data to indicate what the funding requirements of the company might be over the next five-year period.

The forecast sale of the division for $250,000 in Year 2 is uncertain and it might be more appropriate initially to exclude this income from the forecast in order to assess what the maximum funding requirements might be.

The forecast below shows negative cash flows and a requirement for additional funding. Because the company will be making loan repayments in Years 2 and 3, the need for new external finance in the planning period is not at all surprising.

	Year 1 1st 6 mths	Year 1 2nd 6 mths	Year 2 1st 6 mths	Year 2 2nd 6 mths	Year 3	Year 4	Year 5
	$000	$000	$000	$000	$000	$000	$000
Cash in	+290	+260	+308	+266	+615	+635	+650
Cash out	-350	-225	-799	-156	-598	-505	-522
Cash surplus/(deficit) for the period	-60	+35	-491	+110	+17	+130	+128
Opening cash balance	10	-50	-15	-506	-396	-379	-249
Closing cash balance	-50	-15	-506	-396	-379	-249	-121

The total funding requirement as at the end of each period can be shown in the form of a bar chart, as follows.

Total five-year funding requirements

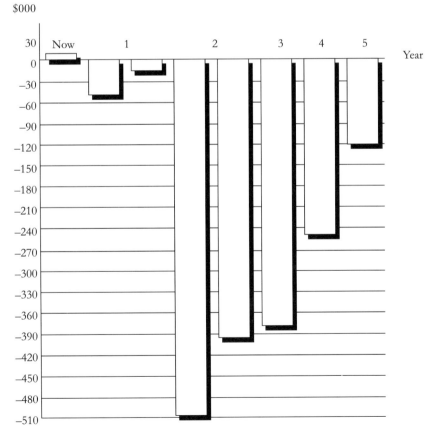

Categorizing Funding Requirements

Having prepared a long-term cash forecast from the company's business plan (strategic plan), financial planners should have a good idea of how much funding the company will require, when and for how long. The planners also should have a realistic view of how reliable the forecasts are. Inevitably, actual cash flows will not match forecasts exactly, and there must be some allowance made for forecasting error. In addition, cash flows from uncertain events, such as cash flows from the possible sale of a division, as illustrated in the example, could make a big difference to funding needs should they actually occur.

Funding requirements can be broken down into three categories:

- long-term (core) funding requirements
- short-term or medium-term funding requirements
- contingency requirements.

Each requirement should be funded in different ways. In other words, the nature of the funding requirement dictates the preferred type of funding. For example, core funding needs as a general rule will be satisfied by equity funding and, if available, long-term debt. Short-term cyclical funding and contingency requirements usually are satisfied by shorter-term bank lines.

Analyzing the total funding needs of the business into these three categories calls for judgment as to which requirements are core and which are cyclical and of short-term or medium-term duration. There is no one correct answer, and much depends on the nature of the company's business. For example, a property investment company might categorize funding to pay for completed property developments as core funding for a long-term asset, while a property development company would categorize the costs of a development as cyclical short- to medium-term funding for an asset it confidently will expect to sell on completion of the development.

Long-Term Core Funding Requirements

The long-term funding requirements of a business are the funds needed to finance its core business assets such as land, buildings and equipment. Every business has core assets, although it is not always readily apparent what they are. For example, the core assets of airline companies at one time were their fleets of aircraft. Now, however, many airlines avoid owning aircraft, preferring to lease them, and their main core assets have become information technology systems and landing slots at airports. Some hotel groups have ceased owning the hotels they manage, and their core assets are the management contracts for hotels that are owned by third parties.

Short/Medium-Term Cyclical Requirements

Most companies are subject to cyclical or seasonal fluctuations in their cash flow, often reflecting a seasonal trading pattern. Department stores, for example, have a trading bias towards the pre-Christmas period and perhaps biannual sales periods. Many energy companies have only a small proportion of their operational cash inflows during the six-month period to September 30 and most of their cash inflows in the six-month winter period.

Even companies with no apparent cyclical influences on cash flow, receiving a relatively constant stream of income, might in reality have a short-term cash flow cycle. They might, for example, accumulate cash receipts at a steady rate throughout each month but make bulk payments (for materials and wages and salaries) only one or two days each month, or just once every quarter (for rent payments). Business cycles, and their associated cash flows, can span several years, for example in the development of agricultural and forestry businesses.

It would be inappropriately expensive to finance assets with equity or long-term debt when periodic rather than continuous funding is required. Cyclical, i.e. temporarily needed funds should be available medium-term or short-term, according to the length of the business cycle.

Forecasting seasonal fluctuations in cash flows is often fairly straightforward. Historical seasonal patterns can be projected forward, with adjustments made for any foreseeable change in business circumstances. Forecasting funding requirements for a business that goes through a long-term cycle of growth and recession calls for much more skill, however. The company has to anticipate the cash needs of the business between the peak, most beneficial point on the cycle and the point of maximum recession in the market.

A key judgment is to establish the worse-case scenario. The worst anticipated outcome should dictate the required level of funding. If the company is relatively immune to the effects of a general economic recession, e.g. a food retailer, the quantification can be fairly easy. If, however, the company is highly sensitive to the economic cycle, e.g. a property development company, it is extremely difficult to judge and forecast cash needs over a long term.

Contingency Requirements

Contingency funds are to meet unexpected requirements. A company should have access to contingency funding for a number of reasons. There could be an unexpected downturn in one of its markets or the opportunity to make an acquisition. The level of contingency funding depends on such factors as:

- the volatility of the markets in which the company operates
- the vulnerability of the earnings stream to market recession
- the dependence on one or just a few major customers for achieving sales targets
- management's desire for growth by making acquisitions.

Contingency funding should be obtained by means of short-term committed bank facilities.

Example

A company has reviewed its estimated total funding requirements for the next ten years in its annual business plan update. Total funding requirements are indicated in the following chart.

Total ten-year funding requirements

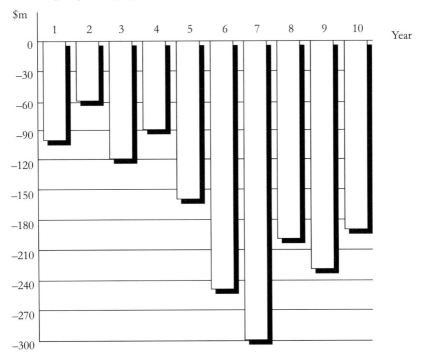

Analysis

The company's management would have to look into the reasons for the overall funding requirement. Judgment is needed to determine how the funding requirement should be met, from long-term or shorter-term funds or bank facilities. A proposed funding policy should be built into the business plan.

Proposal 1

The company might consider, for example, the following policy:

- Raise $100 million in long-term funds in Year 1. Invest any surplus funds in the second and fourth years.
- Meet the extra funding requirements in Year 3 from a medium-term borrowing arrangement, perhaps through a three-year loan of $20 million.

- Raise a further $50 million in long-term funds in Year 5.
- Arrange a five-year bond issue of $150 million in Year 6.

This policy would produce the following funding profile.

Year	New funds obtained	Cumulative extra funding obtained Long term	Med. term	Short term	Total	Funding requirement	Surplus
	$m	$m	$m	$m	$m	$m	$m
1	+100	100	-	-	100	100	0
2	-	100	-	-	100	60	40
3	+20	100	-	20	120	120	0
4	-	100	-	20	120	90	30
5	+50	150	-	20	170	160	10
6	+150-20	150	150	-	300	250	50
7	-	150	150	-	300	300	0
8	-	150	150	-	300	200	100
9	-	150	150	-	300	230	70
10	-	150	150	-	300	190	110

Some extra contingency funding probably would be needed in most of the Years 1 to 7, when extra funding obtained would exceed the amount of funding required by fairly small amounts (ranging from 0 to $50 million).

Proposal 2

This funding policy is by no means ideal, because it results in a large funding surplus in Years 8 to 10. An alternative arrangement is suggested in the table below. This provides for more long-term funding and less medium-term borrowing.

Year	New funds obtained	Cumulative extra funding obtained Long term	Med. term	Short term	Total	Funding requirement	Surplus
	$m	$m	$m	$m	$m	$m	$m
1	+100	100	-	-	100	100	0
2	-	100	-	-	100	60	40
3	+20	120	-	-	120	120	0
4	-	120	-	-	120	90	30
5	+50	120	50	-	170	160	10
6	+60+20	180	50	20	250	250	0
7	+50	180	50	70	300	300	0
8	-70	180	50	-	230	200	30
9	-	180	50	-	230	230	0
10	-50+10	180	-	10	190	190	0

This proposal would involve raising long-term funds three times in the next ten years, in Year 1 ($100 million), Year 3 ($20 million) and Year 6 ($60 million), a five-year medium-term loan of $50 million in Year 5, and short-term funding in years six, seven and 10. Contingency funding arrangements would be required in addition.

Summary

It is essential for large companies to plan funding requirements several years in advance, and to review the plan regularly. Having a funding plan will allow the company's financial managers to monitor the capital markets and the loan markets, and to make funding decisions that:

are consistent with the business plan, but

at the same time take advantage of any windows of opportunity for raising funds on favorable terms.

Funding Options

In the previous chapter, it was suggested that management should make an estimate of the total external funding requirements over the business planning period, and categorize them into long-term, shorter-term and contingency funds. The next stage in the planning process is to decide, in broad terms, how much of the new funds should be raised in the form of equity, how much as debt, and whether hybrid financial instruments should be used for part of the funding.

The choice between equity, debt and hybrid financial instruments is influenced by a variety of factors:

- the cost of each funding option (particularly the cost of equity and the cost of debt capital)
- stock market rating
- operational profits and cash flows
- leverage (financial leverage)
- the purpose for which the funds are required (nature and duration of the funded activities)
- availability
- recent funding measures
- control of the company
- individual preferences.

Cost of Capital

The cost of capital is the average return, over the long term, that investors expect to receive from their investment. It is therefore the average yield that companies should expect to pay. There is the cost of equity stocks, and a cost for each issue of debt capital and each bank loan. Each financial instrument has a different cost to the issuer, and the cost of capital can vary over time, as investor expectations change.

To a company, the overall cost of its funds (debt, equity and hybrid instruments together) is the return its investors expect to receive in the long term, expressed as a percentage annual rate of return. This average cost of funds is commonly referred to as the company's weighted average cost of capital. A company's aim should be, if possible, to minimize its average cost of funds, and raise capital at the cheapest rate possible.

Cost of Equity

The cost of equity capital (ordinary stocks/common stock) is the expected long-term average annual returns to stockholders, expressed as a percentage of the stock price. Returns on equity can be measured in one of two ways:

- as dividends and capital gains from increases in the stock price (or capital losses from stock price falls) or
- as a stream of dividend payments into the future in perpetuity. The stock price at any time is the market's valuation of expected future dividends, and capital gains occur, i.e. the stock price rises when dividend expectations improve.

In the short term, the cost of equity can be zero, because a company's board of directors can decide to pay no dividends. However, not paying a dividend is only a short-term option. There are exceptions, such as NASDAQ biotech start-up companies and the Alternative Investment Market (AIM) in London. Eventually, dividend payments will have to be resumed. A company that has passed, i.e. not paid a recent dividend, could have difficulty raising new equity capital should it require additional funding. Stockholders would have to be assured that high returns could be expected from their further investment in the company.

Equity is usually much more expensive than debt capital. Stockholders expect a high long-term average return to compensate them for the greater risk factor in their investment. The main risk for stockholders arises from the unpredictable nature of their annual income that can fluctuate from one year to the next. Actual profits and therefore dividends could turn out to be much lower than expected, giving disappointing returns in some years.

Unlike providers of debt capital who have a right to interest payments (and the repayment of the debt principal) stockholders rely on the discretion and judgment of the company's executice officers for their dividend income.

An estimate can be made of the cost of equity for each company quoted on a stock market. There are, however, some important reservations.

- When the cost of equity is based on expectations of future dividends, deciding the expected rate of dividend growth can be a matter of informed guesswork and judgment.
- The cost of equity is also based on the stock's market price. The market for the stocks should be liquid, otherwise the current market price might be unrealistic and distorted by a temporary shortage of demand or supply in the market. The current market price is also the price at which stocks are being offered for sale at a specific time, not the price at which existing stockholders originally bought their stocks.

Given these qualifications, there are two main methods of estimating the cost of a company's equity:

- the Gordon dividend growth model
- the capital-asset pricing model.

The Gordon Dividend Growth Model

An alternative method of measuring the cost of a company's equity stocks is a dividend growth model. This model is based on the assumption that a stock price reflects the market's current valuation of expected future dividends (in perpetuity) from the stock. This valuation is related to

- the annual returns or yield that stockholders expect to receive from the stock over time, and
- expectations of future growth in dividends over time.

The stock price is the present value of expected future dividends, discounted at the stockholders' required annual yield.

Given the stock price and an estimate of expected future dividends, the model can be used to estimate the cost of equity capital. To keep the arithmetic simple, we shall assume that the anticipated annual growth in dividends is a constant percentage amount. The dividend growth model states that the cost of equity, i.e. the expected average annual yield from a stock, is as follows:

$$r = \frac{d(1+g)}{MV} + g$$

Where:

- r is the cost of equity, as a proportion, e.g. 5% = 0.05, 12% = 0.12
- MV is the stock's current market price (ex div)
- d is the most recent annual dividend
- g is the expected annual growth in dividends, expressed as a proportion.

In the formula, $d(1 + g)$ is therefore the expected dividend for the forthcoming year.

Example
A company's treasury department is trying to establish the cost of the company's equity. The current annual dividend is 10.8 cents per stock, and the stock's market price has averaged 270 cents over the past few days. It is estimated that stockholders are expecting annual dividend payments to increase by 2% in real terms, that is 2% above the rate of inflation. Inflation is currently expected to average 4% per year in perpetuity, and dividends are therefore expected to rise by 6% per annum.

Analysis

Using the dividend growth model, an estimate of the company's current cost of equity would be as follows.

$$r = \frac{10.8\ (1.06)}{270} + 0.06$$

$$= 0.0424 + 0.06$$

$$= 0.1024 \text{ or } 10.24\% \text{ p.a.}$$

Capital-Asset Pricing Model

The capital-asset pricing model (CAPM) is a mathematical model for estimating the expected average returns from individual stocks (or a portfolio of stocks).

The model, in broad outline, is based on a comparison of:

- the yield available on risk-free investments (long-term domestic government bonds)
- the average market yield, i.e. the comparable average returns from the stock market as a whole. This is usually, but not always, higher than the risk-free investment yield
- the yield on the stocks of an individual company. This could be higher or lower than the average market yield, depending on whether the stocks are high-risk or low-risk.

The yield from stocks is measured as the dividend during a period, plus the increase in the stock price or minus the fall in the stock price. The dividend and the capital gain in the period, taken together, can be measured as an annual percentage yield on the stock price.

Over time, the capital-asset pricing model can be used to measure and monitor changes in the market yield and the comparable change in the yield on individual stocks. From the analysis, it is possible to predict by how much the yield on a particular stock might rise or fall, given a rise or fall in the average market yield.

The size of the yield from stocks of an individual company depends, however, on two groups of factors:

- those that are specific or special to the company, for example the quality of its management. These factors give rise to specific or unsystematic risk.
- those that affect all firms in the economy, to a greater or lesser extent, and not just the individual company. These factors give rise to market risk or systematic risk.

The yield on a stock therefore depends on a mixture of factors that are specific to the company and factors that affect the economy and the market as a whole. An investor can overcome the problems of specific risk by diversifying his/her investments, and holding a well-balanced portfolio of stocks (an efficient portfolio). In any period some stocks will perform better than expected because of specific factors, and others will perform badly. In an efficient portfolio the stocks performing well will balance the stocks performing badly.

Market risk (systematic risk) cannot be eliminated by diversifying investments. When the market as a whole improves, individual stocks should also yield bigger returns. When the market performs badly, most individual stocks will perform badly also.

The CAPM is used to establish the systematic risk for stocks in individual companies, and to assess the return that an investor with an efficient portfolio of investments should expect to receive from his stocks. This expected yield (ignoring specific risk factors) should determine the company's cost of capital and its market price.

The CAPM Formula

The CAPM formula for the expected return on an individual stock is as follows:

$$R_s = R_{rf} + \beta(R_m - R_{rf})$$

Where:

- R_s is the expected return on an individual stock

- R_{rf} is the rate of return on risk-free investments
- R_m is the average market rate of return
- $(R_m - R_{rf})$ is therefore the difference between the average stock market yield and the yield on risk-free investments. This is sometimes known as the excess market yield or the equity risk premium.
- ß, the beta factor, is explained below.

To determine the expected return on an individual stock, the excess yield is multiplied by a beta factor. Each stock has its own beta factor, established from a comparative analysis over time of market yields and yields on the stock.

When ß = 1, the expected return is the same as the average market return. The beta factor for the stock market as a whole is therefore 1. You can work this out by inserting ß = 1 in the CAPM formula:

$$R_s = R_{rf} + 1(R_m - R_{rf})$$

$$= R_{rf} + R_m - R_{rf}$$

$$R_s = R_m$$

When ß = 0, the expected return is the risk-free yield. The beta factor of risk-free securities is 0. Again, you can work this out by inserting ß = 0 in the formula:

$$R_s = R_{rf} + 0(R_m - R_{rf})$$

$$R_s = R_{rf}$$

When a stock's beta factor is between nought and one, its risk is lower than for the stock market as a whole. When average market returns rise or fall, returns from the stock should rise or fall by a lower amount. Low beta factors are associated with defensive stocks.

When a stock's beta factor is greater than one, its specific risk is greater than for the stock market as a whole. When average market returns rise or fall, returns from the stock should rise or fall by a larger amount. High beta factors are associated with cyclical stocks.

Example
Stocks of Foxtrot have a beta factor of 0.8 and stocks of Golf have a beta factor of 1.1. The risk-free rate of return is 7% and the average stock market return is 12%.

Analysis
The expected yield from Foxtrot stocks, applying the CAPM formula, is

7% + 0.8(12% - 7%) = 11%. This is less than the average stock market yield.

If the average market return rises to 14%, and the risk-free yield remains 7%, the expected yield on Foxtrot's stocks will rise to: 7% + 0.8(14% - 7%) = 12.6%.

A 2% increase in the average market return, from 12% to 14%, results in an increase of 1.6%(0.8 x 2%) in the expected return on Foxtrot stocks, from 11% to 12.6%.

The expected yield from Golf stocks that have a beta factor in excess of one, is 7% + 1.1(12% - 7%) = 12.5%. This is higher than the average stock market yield. If the average market return rises by 2% to 14%, and the risk-free yield remains at 7%, the expected yield on Golf stocks will rise by 2.2% (1.1 x 2%) to 7% + 1.1(14% - 7%) = 14.7%.

An implication of CAPM analysis is that raising new equity could be very expensive for companies that have high-risk (cyclical) businesses. However, the optimal time for raising new equity would be

- when returns on all investments are fairly low, and
- near the bottom of the economic cycle, when the difference between the average stock market return and the risk-free rate of return is quite small.

Obtaining Beta Factors

Beta factors for quoted companies are calculated and kept up-to-date by stock market analysts and academics. In the US, Barra Associates publishes beta factors for companies in a number of countries. In the UK, a widely publicized model is maintained and published by the London Business School. In addition, financial database operators such as Reuters and Bloomberg calculate betas.

- The comparative cost of equity and debt capital can affect a company's choice between equity and debt funding.
- Investment projects funded by new equity capital should be expected to earn a return (over the project's life) in excess of the funding cost.

Cost of Debt Capital

Normally debt capital will cost less than equity for two reasons.

- The returns from an investment in bonds or from a loan are predictable (provided the borrower is creditworthy). With a fixed-rate loan, repayments are scheduled, known amounts. With a variable-rate loan, the lender can expect to receive interest at a known margin above a benchmark rate of interest, e.g. at 1% above LIBOR, the London Interbank Offered Rate.
- Interest payments on debt are allowable expenses, usually for the purpose of assessing a company's tax liability. Dividend payments on stocks, in contrast, are not allowable, and are paid out of post-tax income.

To compare the cost of equity and debt capital for a profitable company, it is therefore appropriate to adjust the cost of debt to allow for the offsetting reduction in tax payments. The after-tax cost of debt is the pre-tax cost of the interest payments multiplied by a factor $(1 - t)$, where t is the rate of tax payable on profits.

Example
A company's pre-tax cost of debt is 10% per annum, and the company pays tax on its profits at a rate of 30%.

Analysis

The company's after-tax cost of debt is 7%, the pre-tax cost of 10% multiplied by a factor of
(1-0.30).

Weighted Average Cost of Existing Debt Capital

An average cost of debt can be calculated for the cost of each item of debt capital in a company's funding structure. The average should be weighted, to allow for differing amounts of each item of debt.

The pre-tax cost of a bank loan is the rate of interest currently payable. The pre-tax cost of a market debt instrument (e.g. a bond) is its current gross yield to redemption.

Example

A company has the following debt items in its funding structure:

- a $20 million drawing on an overdraft facility, with interest at base rate plus 1%
- a $50 million term bank loan at a fixed interest rate of 8.2%
- a $20 million drawing on a bilateral bank facility, with interest payable at three-month LIBOR + 50 basis points (50bp)
- a $30 million term loan at a variable rate of three-month LIBOR + 20 basis points (20bp)
- a $20 million issue of sterling Bankers Acceptances (short-term promissory notes) at one-month LIBOR flat.

Current benchmark interest rates are:

Base rates	7%
One-month LIBOR	6.50%
Three-month LIBOR	6.75%

Analysis

The weighted average pre-tax cost of debt (WACD) for the company currently is as follows:

Item	Amount	Cost	Weighting (amount x cost)
	$m		$m
Overdraft	20	0.0800	1.600
Term loan (fixed rate)	50	0.0820	4.100
Bilateral facility	20	0.0725	1.450
Term loan (variable rate)	30	0.0695	2.085
Sterling Bas	20	0.0650	1.300
	140		10.535

$$\text{Pre-tax WACD} = \frac{10.535}{140} \quad \text{x} \quad 100\% \quad = 7.525\%$$

If the company pays tax at 30%, the post-tax WACD would be 5.27% (7.525 multiplied by a factor of 0.70).

The WACD figure will change whenever any of the component parts of the debt portfolio change, e.g. if the amount of the overdraft changes, or if there is a rise of fall in the reference LIBOR rates or base rate.

A company might use either a weighted average cost of debt or the specific cost of new debt to measure the cost of the debt capital. The method chosen will be determined by the attitude of the company to debt funding, i.e. whether funding requirements are met

- out of a general corporate pot that is topped up periodically, in which case a weighted average cost of debt is an appropriate measure, or
- by arranging discrete debt funding for each new project in which case the cost of the specific debt is the appropriate measure.

Specific Cost of New Debt

A specific cost can be estimated, taking into account general market conditions, and the current yields payable on different types of debt instrument and for loans of different maturities. However, the cost of new debt capital will of course vary according to the size and creditworthiness of the company.

The cost of raising new debt should include the interest rate or yield payable, and also any front-end arrangement fees or commitment fees. For example, a one-year bank facility might be obtainable at 12-month LIBOR plus 75 basis points (0.75%) plus a commitment fee of 25 basis points. If 12-month LIBOR is currently 8%, the full cost of the facility would be 9% (8% + 0.75% + 0.25%).

The pre-tax cost of raising new debt capital should be the cheapest funding method obtainable that fits the company's requirements for maturity, i.e. the funding period. For example, if a company needs to raise debt capital with a five-year maturity, it might compare the expected costs of a five-year bank loan and a five-year bond.

Stock Market Rating

A company will prefer to raise new equity funds when these are relatively cheap, i.e. when the stock price is high relative to the market. Stock prices are influenced by the perceptions and opinions of investors and stock market analysts. These might differ from the perceptions of the management, who might believe that the stocks are either overvalued or undervalued.

Companies are unlikely to issue new equity when management believes the stock price is undervalued, either because of a general fall in stock market prices or because the stocks are cheap compared with those of other companies in the industry or business sector. A concern would be that issuing new stocks when the price is low could be earnings-dilutive. If the stock price seems low and the company needs to raise new finance, it might therefore opt for debt capital rather than equity.

Operational Profits and Cash flows

Debt involves an obligation by the borrower to make payments of interest and to repay the debt principal, according to an agreed payment schedule.

If a company is unable to make a scheduled payment on a debt, it will be exposed to the risk of action by the lender to recover the debt. In an extreme case, the company could be forced into liquidation by the lender.

With equity capital, in contrast, there is no requirement to pay dividends. Stockholders cannot put their own company into liquidation for failing to pay a dividend, although non-payment of dividends to preferred stockholders could in some cases give these stockholders more voting rights in the company. A company with uncertain or volatile profits and cash flows should rely more extensively on equity finance, and should structure the balance sheet to contain only as much debt it can support.

Example 1
In June 1998 London and Continental Railways, the builder of the £5.8bn Channel tunnel rail link, announced plans to part-finance the project through an equity issue to new investors. In order to encourage investors, who would be deterred by the long delay before LCR was expected to generate profits, LCR agreed that equity investors would have eligibility for tax relief on their own profits – effectively, selling LCR's future tax losses. Losses were expected to amount to £600-700 million before the project moved to profit.

Lenders can try to insist that a borrower's profits or cash flows are sufficient to cover interest charges on lending. This requirement is implicit, for example, in a standard covenant on many bank loans, that the profits of the borrower must exceed interest costs by a minimum multiple amount, e.g. by at least 2.5 times. An interest cover covenant makes it an event of default for the borrower's profit before tax and interest (PBIT) to fall below the stipulated multiple of interest payments.

Example 2
The risks of taking on excessive debt even for a profitable company were clear in the case of Autos Inc, a small listed used-car dealer.

In the first half of 1997, the company announced interim profits that had increased over the previous years. At the time book leverage (sheet debt/stockholders' funds) stood at 175% but interest cover was three times, that was seen to be in line with projections. However, lower demand for used vehicles and a subsequent decline in both sales and margins in the second half led to a profit warning in July 1998 that indicated a loss, thus wiping out interest cover. As a result, the company's stock price fell 37% in the week following the warning, further increasing the company's leverage.

A business review identified a need to reduce the break-even point of the business, and to restructure its external financing through an injection of additional equity.

A prudent financial manager will set the debt component of the company's capital structure at a level that can be serviced in the worst case event of a fall in profits and a rise in interest rates. To judge the maximum tolerable debt level, consistent with profits and cash flows, calls for

- an estimate of core profitability, the level of sustainable profit achievable at the lowest point in the business cycle, and
- an estimate of the maximum anticipated interest rates.

By making worst-case assumptions about sales, costs and interest rates, the company's business plan can be redrawn, and a worst-case level of cash flows measured. From these estimates, the company can judge the maximum amount of debt that could be borne without risking failure to repay because of insufficient profits and cash flows.

Leverage

The financial leverage level of a company is the relative proportion of debt to equity in the company's capital structure.

Financial leverage can be measured in several ways. Broadly, however, there are two basic methods.

Method 1

$$G = \frac{D}{E} \times 100\%$$

Method 2

$$G = \frac{D}{D+E} \times 100\%$$

Where:

- G is the leverage level expressed as a percentage
- D is debt (short and long term)
- E is equity.

Debt and equity can be either at balance sheet values or at market values. A leverage ratio can be measured both for groups of companies as a whole, and for individual companies.

Method 1 is more commonly used by stock market analysts, so that a company's leverage is 100% when its debt capital is equal in amount/value to its equity capital.

Example
In its 1998 accounts, Alpha Holdings Group Inc reported the following figures in its balance sheet:

	Group as a whole	Holding company only
	$m	$m
Loans, overdrafts and HP		
Due within one year	259.3	99.1
Due after one year	741.7	231.2
Less cash balances	(163.5)	(81.5)
	837.5	248.8
Capital and reserves	261.2	626.1
	1,098.7	874.9

Analysis
The leverage ratio of the group and the holding company could be measured as follows:

Group:	$\dfrac{837.5}{261.2}$	x 100%	320%
Holding company:	$\dfrac{248.8}{626.1}$	x 100%	40%

These ratios indicate that as a group Alpha was highly leveraged. However, given the strong growth prospects of the company, its stable interest cover at 3.7 times and its good asset backing, the debt markets and loan providers regarded these ratios as acceptable.

The Significance of Leverage

A high level of leverage implies greater financial risk for both lenders and stockholders.

- The risk to lenders is that a company with large debts might be unable to meet its repayment obligations in full and on schedule.
- The risk to stockholders is greater volatility in profits, and a greater possibility of fluctuating dividends.

Example

A company valued at $300 million suffers a 20% fall in profits before interest and tax from $40 million to $32 million. The company is highly leveraged, with debt capital of $200 million and equity of $100 million. The average cost of its debt capital is 10%. Taxation on profits is at the rate of 30%.

Analysis

Income before interest and tax (PBIT) have fallen by 20%, but the profits for stockholders have fallen by a much greater percentage amount.

	Previous	Current
	$m	$m
PBIT	40	32
Interest (10% x £200m)	(20)	(20)
Income before tax	20	12
Tax (30%)	(6)	(3.6)
Income after tax	14	8.4

Income for stockholders has fallen by 40% from $14 million to $8.4 million.

If the company had lower leverage, with debt of $100 million and equity of $200 million, the percentage fall in income for stockholders would have been smaller.

	Previous	**Current**
	$m	$m
PBIT	40	32
Interest (10% x $100m)	(10)	(10)
Income before tax	30	22
Tax (30%)	(9)	(6.6)
Income after tax	21	15.4

The fall in after-tax income is just 27%, down from $21 million to $15.4 million.

Stockholders facing higher risk, i.e. a greater volatility in earnings (and dividends), will expect a higher return as compensation for the risk. The cost of equity funding therefore will be higher.

Restraints on the Leverage Level

Formal constraints can be applied by means of covenants on existing loans, or by the company's articles of incorporation. One of the most common loan covenants is a restriction on the company's ability to borrow in relation to the value of its equity or stockholders' funds, i.e. stock capital and reserves. Typically, there is a limitation that debt be no more than about 150% or 175% of equity. However, most companies would be in serious financial difficulties if the level of debt neared the maximum permitted by a loan covenant.

The financial markets (investors and analysts) often will look unfavorably on companies with more debt than equity in their capital structure, although there are exceptions where much higher leverage is normal, e.g. banks and property companies.

Informal constraints on leverage levels are applied by stockholders or more often company management.

- Management often will establish a limit on the level of leverage they will be prepared to sanction, in order to cap the financial risk and minimize the likelihood of the company ever defaulting on its loan obligations.
- Management might also fear the consequences of high leverage on the stock market valuation of the company's stocks.

Leverage and Commercial Risks

Corporate profitability depends to a large extent on the commercial risks of the company's businesses. When commercial risk is high, profits will be subject to greater fluctuations and uncertainty.

Commercial risk exists when a company is exposed to:

- business cycles in the market
- the risk of technological change and product obsolescence, i.e. a rapid pace of technological change in the industry
- risks from competition
- price sensitivity of the market, i.e. to changes in the prices of the company's products
- the risk of government intervention or legislation affecting the company's business.

It was explained earlier that a high financial leverage level exposes a company's stockholders to the risk of volatile earnings. This risk will be much higher when the company is exposed to significant commercial risks.

Operational Leverage

Commercial risk can be particularly high in companies with high operating leverage. Operating leverage refers to the cost structure of a company's operations, and the way in which income changes with an increase or decrease in sales.

Operations have low leverage when fixed costs are fairly low, but variable costs are relatively high as a proportion of sales. As a consequence,

- fixed costs are covered at a fairly low volume of sales, i.e. breakeven is at a fairly low volume of sales
- the net income margin is relatively low, and the change in total income for each $1 increase or decrease in sales is fairly low
- operating income therefore tends to be fairly stable despite changes in turnover from one year to the next.

High operating leverage occurs when a company has relatively high fixed costs, and relatively low variable costs, so that the change in profit for every $1 increase or decrease in sales is high. As a consequence,

- a high volume of sales is needed just to breakeven and cover fixed costs
- profits change sharply when sales rise or fall, and tend to fluctuate sharply in the business cycle of growth and recession.

A company exposed to high commercial risk should opt for a low level of financial risk (financial leverage), to reduce the risk of failure and to protect stockholders from excessively volatile returns.

Commercial risk	Financial risk (leverage)	Comment
HIGH	LOW	New funding requirements should be met by a mixture of debt and equity that keeps leverage levels quite low
HIGH	HIGH	A high-risk company. The cost of any new funding could be high. An equity issue (or retained profits) would be needed to reduce financial risk
LOW	LOW	New funding requirements could be met by debt capital, without exposing the company to excessive risk
LOW	HIGH	High financial leverage is more acceptable when commercial risks are low

In contrast, a company with low commercial risk could increase the financial risk, i.e. increase financial leverage by raising new capital in the form of debt. If the return on new investments by such a company exceeds the cost of new debt, the income for equity stockholders will be enhanced.

There are some exceptions to the rule of avoiding high leverage when commercial risk is high. These include aircraft leasing companies and property development companies that sometimes deliberately combine high commercial risk and high leverage to generate extra profits.

Losses and Leverage

Loss-making companies suffer a reduction in equity capital. A loss-making company must either obtain new finance or suffer a long-term reduction in capital and assets. In the long term, the company must expect a return to profitability, and can hope to rebuild equity through retained profits. Without the prospect of a return to profits, there would be no reason to continue in business. In the short term, however, the reduction in equity capital could have serious repercussions, because financial leverage will rise. Quite possibly, the company will breach loan covenants as a result of losses, and consequently be exposed to action by its bankers or bondholders.

Example

Japanese general contractors typically have high levels of borrowings to finance the construction cycle. Such companies were severely affected by the 1998 Asian crisis that led to an unexpected decline in home starts, capital investments and public spending.

In the summer of 1998 Asakawagumi Co, a Japanese regional construction company, collapsed under a mountain of debt as its main lender refused to grant it further loans. Following five years of losses, funded by increasing bank borrowing, it had net liabilities of ¥20 billion and its stock price fell to below its par value. As it filed for court protection from creditors it became the fourth Japanese listed contractor to collapse since the beginning of 1997.

Purpose of Funding

The duration of a specific project for which funds are required should have a powerful influence on the type of funding. Long-term projects are more likely to be regarded as core businesses that should be financed by equity or long-term debt.

A general rule for the appropriate type of funding for different types of project is as follows:

Funding needs

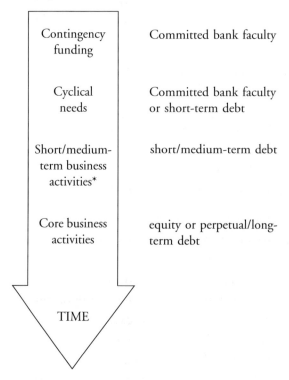

Contingency funding	Committed bank faculty
Cyclical needs	Committed bank faculty or short-term debt
Short/medium-term business activities*	short/medium-term debt
Core business activities	equity or perpetual/long-term debt

TIME

*Businesses with five- to seven-year payback

Stockholders and investors in general dislike opportunistic stock or bond issues by companies. They expect to see an economic case for an issue and are wary of companies that ask for money without clear reasons.

Prevailing Market Conditions

Given that the stock price for new equity issues has to be set at a level that will attract investors, market conditions can be an important factor in any decision to raise capital by issuing new equity or debt instruments. Issuing new equity can be a high-risk exercise in a bear market, when stock prices are falling.

Equity issues are generally in the form of a rights issue to existing stockholders, new stocks have to be offered at a discount to the stock price. As a general guide, the offer price for stocks in a rights issue should be at a discount of about 10-15% of the theoretical ex-rights price, when the issue is underwritten.

The announcement of a rights issue occasionally can generate market fears that the company is in trading difficulties or faces a critical shortage of funds. As a consequence, investors might see no compelling economic case for the issue. There could be heavy selling of the company's stocks in the stock market, to the extent that the issue soon ceases to be priced at a deep discount and becomes an at-the-money issue, i.e. with new stocks offered at the price to which the existing stocks have fallen.

A new stock issue can be underwritten. In return for a commission, underwriters, who are usually stockholders in the company, agree to buy up to a certain quantity of the stocks at the issue price if there is insufficient demand from other buyers. Although a company can guarantee selling its stocks to underwriters, it is nevertheless important to secure a high percentage take-up of the new stocks by existing stockholders, in order to have a successful issue. If an issue is unsuccessful, the stock price will remain depressed because of expectations that unwanted stocks will be sold in the market whenever the price begins to rise.

Market conditions also can affect a company's ability to raise new debt capital in the form of bonds, notes, commercial paper or hybrid instruments, e.g. convertible bonds or preferred stocks. Demand for new paper in different domestic and international markets can vary over time, and opportunities can exist, briefly, to issue new securities at a favourable (low) yield.

Example
Fiat, the Italian car-making group, has in the past obtained medium- and long-term debt funding by occasionally issuing (unrated) bonds or medium-term notes (MTNs) in the euromarkets. Borrowing costs on eurobonds and euroMTNs generally have been lower than for bank loans. The company also found that borrowing in the euromarkets (with standard euromarket documentation) was easier and quicker than borrowing from banks that would impose more onerous loan covenants and documentation requirements.

From 1992, however, the heavy borrowing requirements of many governments, notably the UK, US, Germany and Italy, the devaluation of the lira, and the financial difficulties of several other Italian organisations, e.g. EFIM, made it very difficult for Fiat to continue using the euromarkets. As a result, the group was forced to turn to syndicated bank loans for the first time in several years.

Recent Funding Measures

Large companies often seek to raise new debt finance regularly. However, there are limits to how often any company can tap the same market for new funds. Large issues of equity, for example, might be acceptable every three to four years. Having made one large debt issue, a company therefore should wait some time before making another. If it needs extra funds, it should look to alternative types and sources of funding.

In contrast, equity issues can be made regularly, provided they are not earnings-dilutive. If a company makes equity issues regularly there could be concern as to the best means of avoiding earnings dilution.

Control of the Company

All types of funding involve some loss of management control. A new stock issue can prompt stockholders to voice dissatisfaction with the company's management, if they believe the issue to be unnecessary and unjustified. Criticisms can create a restraint on future management actions. When new stocks are issued, they can find their way to new and more demanding investors.

New issues of debt capital, or new bank loans, can restrict management control though the imposition of loan covenants that can constrain the company from new borrowing or asset disposals, for example.

Conclusion

Because a company's preference for equity or debt capital can be influenced by a variety of factors, it might be useful to show how several of these factors combine to influence a new funding decision.

Example
A publishing group announced a new equity issue (a one-for-five rights issue) to raise $190 million. The stock market valuation of the company's equity at the time was about $1.1 billion. However, the balance sheet value of equity was about $170 million only, and on this basis of measurement, leverage was high, at about 180%. One of the aims of the issue was to use the equity finance to pay off some of the group's debt, then about $300 million. A second reason was to acquire a war chest for future acquisitions.

Analysis
The company's finance director acknowledged that the main purpose of the issue was to strengthen the company's balance sheet, and reduce the leverage level.

A consequence of the issue, however, was that the company would be using equity to replace cheap borrowings. The cash war chest would be earning only a low rate of interest, and the company's earnings per stock would suffer a dilution of about 10%.

A stock analyst commented that the company had taken an opportunity to issue new stocks when the current stock price was high and stock market investors would probably be willing to support the issue.

Equity

There must be some equity in every company. An important issue in capital structure planning, however, is

- how much equity there should be, and
- what the source (or sources) of new equity should be.

All-Equity Companies

Some companies are able to finance their activities entirely from internally generated cash flows. Typically, their business operations are cash cows, and there is not much need for capital to finance new investments and growth. There is more cash coming into the business than the company needs to spend.

Cash-rich businesses face the problem of what to do with their spare cash. They can hold on to the cash, expecting to use it at some time in the future, for example to finance an acquisition. Until required, the cash can be reinvested to earn interest. When interest rates are very high, holding cash can be earnings enhancing because interest yields could be higher than the profit ratios on normal business activities. When interest rates are low, however, holding cash can be earnings-dilative, because interest yields are much lower than operational profit margins. At these times, cash-rich companies could become embarrassed by their liquidity, and could have too much cash. As a consequence, some cash-rich companies might raise the level of dividend payouts to stockholders and have a low dividend cover. Dividend cover is the ratio of after-tax profits to dividends.

Occasionally public companies might, subject to legal requirements, buy back their stocks in the market and cancel them. This occurs when companies believe that the best use of their money is to give it to stockholders, tacit admission that the company is becoming ex-growth. Buying back stocks and canceling them should have the effect of reducing the company's long-term finance and also improving earnings per stock.

All-equity companies with surplus cash do not necessarily have an optimal capital structure. When interest rates are low, it could benefit such companies to reduce their equity capital. However, senior management might refuse to consider such a move because it could be an admission that they do not know how to use the money at their disposal for further business development.

Equity and Risk

Equity finance can be the only source of new funds for companies that are financially weak and have a low credit rating.

Example
In 1998 an international music, video and CD-ROM publisher and distributor announced an open offer and subscription supported by an underwriting agreement and personal guarantees. The proposals were conditional upon stockholders' approval, but the company announced that if stockholders did not vote in favor of the resolution and the proposals were not implemented, the directors believed that their bankers would provide no new banking facilities. This would leave the company in a position where it would have insufficient working capital and therefore would be unable to continue to trade.

New Equity and the Stock Price

A decision whether or not to seek new long-term capital by issuing stocks can be influenced by the stock rating. When the stock price is high, equity is relatively cheap, and issuing fewer stocks can raise the desired quantity of capital. As a consequence, there is a much lower risk of earnings dilution. The effect on earnings per stock is a critical issue for stockholders/investors.

Example

In 1993, food and tobacco manufacturer RJR Nabisco, announced plans to raise $1.5 billion by issuing 93 million shares. These were to be pegged to the performance of the group's food division, and not the tobacco division, although there would be no legal separation of RJR's tobacco and food divisions. The purpose of the equity issue was to reduce the group's debt that stood at about $14 billion.

The planned issue was abandoned in June 1993 because of the fall in US stock prices for tobacco companies. Stock prices in this sector fell after the start of a tobacco price war in April, when Philip Morris cut the price of Marlboro, its leading cigarette brand.

As a result, RJR Nabisco was unable to obtain the price it wanted for the new stocks. The benefits of lower gearing and lower interest costs were now outweighed by the high cost of the equity. The dividend payments on the new stocks would probably have cost the company almost $200 million annually.

Retained Profits or New Equity?

External funds must come from new stock issues or new borrowings. It was suggested in the chapter on quantifying funding needs (Chapter 2) that a company should forecast its external funding requirements over its business planning period, after allowing for estimates of future profits and dividends. However, retained earnings are by far the most important source of new equity. However, the amount of profits a company can retain is restricted by

- the amount of its after-tax profits, and
- its dividend policy.

Dividend Policy

In an ideal world, a company should achieve growth in both profits and dividends every year. In reality, profits can fall from one year to the next, or turn into losses. A problem for companies with falling profits, as well as for loss-making companies, is to decide whether to maintain dividend payments at the same level as those of the previous year, or to reduce the dividend below last year's level or even pass a dividend entirely, i.e. pay no dividend.

Dividend policy varies between countries. In the US companies on the whole have shown a willingness to reduce dividends when profits fall. By contrast, in the UK for example, reducing the dividend, or paying no dividend, often has been regarded as a sign of severe financial weakness. Therefore companies have been reluctant to cut dividends so long as they have distributable reserves and cash available.

The main argument in favor of maintaining dividend payments is to reassure stockholders about prospects for the future. Dividends are a very important signal to stockholders about the company's prospects, and a dividend cut is an admission by a company of the extent of the serious difficulties it is facing.

Example

A company with 500 million stocks in issue made profits after tax last year of $100 million, and paid a dividend of $50 million. The dividend cover (ratio of distributable profits to dividends) was 2.0 times (100 ÷ 50). The stock price is $2.50.

This year, the company has just announced a fall in profit to $40 million. It will have to make an equity issue in the next few weeks after declaring a dividend for the year. For simplicity, it can be assumed that this is the only dividend for the year. If the dividend is $20 million, keeping the dividend cover at 2.0 times, the company will wish to raise $150 million.

If the dividend is maintained at $50 million, the company will wish to raise $180 million.

Analysis
The company's dividend policy could have a crucial effect on the planned new equity issue because of its effect on stockholders' expectations for the future. A critical consideration is the effect on the stock price of

- paying a reduced dividend of $20 million, and
- paying an uncovered dividend, i.e. a dividend larger than the annual profit, of $50 million.

Experience suggests that the stock price will be more firm if the dividend is maintained.

- Suppose that the dividend is $50 million, and because it is not covered by profits, the stock price falls to $2.25. To raise $180 million, the company would have to issue about 80 million new stocks ($180 million ÷ $2.25).
- Suppose that the dividend is cut to $20 million, and as a consequence the stock price falls to $1.75. To raise $150 million, the company would have to issue about 85 million stocks ($150 million ÷ $1.75).

Issuing fewer stocks would be preferable, to prevent an unnecessary dilution of earnings per stock. In this example, a policy of maintaining the dividend would be a better option than cutting the dividend, because

- it would keep the stock price higher, and equity therefore would be cheaper
- it would be better for the funding of the company to raise the required new capital by issuing fewer stocks
- the current year's dividend to existing stockholders would be maintained at the previous year's level, rather than cut.

In a different situation, cutting the dividend could be better than a policy of maintaining dividends.

Scrip Dividends

On occasion, a company might offer a scrip dividend as an alternative to a cash dividend. A scrip dividend is a dividend paid in the form of new stocks. For example, a company with stocks currently priced at $2 might declare a dividend of 10¢, with a scrip dividend alternative of one new stock for every 20 stocks held. The cash dividend on 20 stocks of $2 (20 x 10¢) and the scrip dividend on 20 stocks (one new stock at a price of $2) would have the same value.

Scrip dividends are a policy option for companies

- with poor cash flows, wishing to reduce the cash dividend payout
- that nevertheless wish to maintain or to increase the dividend per stock.

Scrip dividends allow companies to pay a higher dividend, avoid cash outflows and increase the permanent funding of the company.

Raising New Equity

A company can raise new equity in various ways. The main methods are:

- an initial public offering (IPO) or offer for sale
- a placing or placement
- a rights issue
- by acquiring a subsidiary in exchange for stocks.

Some stocks are also issued through stock option schemes and scrip dividend payments.

Public Offerings

A public offering is the offer of new stocks for sale to the general investing public. This is a common method of stock issue. An offer for sale can involve both

the sale of existing stocks, so that existing holders are simply selling their stocks on the market. This is a common method of achieving an exit for venture capital investors, where the rationale for the IPO is achieving a market for the investors' stocks rather than raising new capital, and

the offer of new stocks to the market, so that the company is raising new equity finance.

Placing

A placing or placement is the sale of stocks by means of selective marketing to a restricted, targeted group of investors, e.g. institutional investors.

Example 1

In July 1998 Coca-Cola Amatil of Australia spun off its central and eastern European businesses and merged them with the Coca-Cola bottling operations in Italy. It then floated the stocks of the new business on the London and Australian stock exchanges through an institutional placing. The offering was over-subscribed 10 times, mainly because of demand from European institutions.

When private companies bring their stocks to the market, the stocks might be sold by combining a placing with a limited public offering.

Example 2

In May 1998 Groupe Flo, the French restaurant chain, offered stocks on the Second Market in Paris in an IPO through an institutional placing and a retail offer. The retail offer was 122 times subscribed – a record for the market.

Rights Issues

A rights issue is a form of stock issue that gives existing stockholders the first refusal on new stocks issued by a company. It is a method of issuing stocks that protects the legal pre-emption rights of existing stockholders. These rights give existing stockholders the first refusal on new stocks issued by the company. A company with 100 million stocks in issue, for example, wishing to issue 20 million new stocks, must offer the new stocks to existing stockholders in a one for five (20 for 100) rights issue. Each stockholder would be entitled to subscribe for one new stock for every five stocks already held. A rights issue is usually underwritten, so that underwriters will purchase new stocks not taken up by existing stockholders at the offer price.

Stockholders can vote to waive their pre-emption rights, and allow the company to issue stocks to new stockholders. This is necessary, for example, when new stocks are issued to acquire a subsidiary, or to establish an executive stock option scheme.

A rights issue is the most common method of increasing the issued stock capital of a public company. The size of a rights issue is limited only by market demand for the company's stocks.

A feature of rights issues is that the offer price of the new stocks is at a discount to the current market price when the issue is announced. The discounted price is intended to encourage stockholders to take up the stocks offered to them.

Pricing a rights issue is difficult when market conditions are unstable. In normal circumstances an issue could be made at a discount of between 10% to 25% to the market price, at the time the issue is announced.

The theoretical ex-rights price is the weighted average price of the stocks before the rights issue is announced, and the new stocks. In theory, this is the stock price that should be expected after the issue takes place.

Example
A company whose stock price is currently $3 announces a one-for-three rights issue, with the new stocks to be issued at $2.48 each.

Analysis
The theoretical ex-rights price is an average price, calculated as follows:

	$
Three old stocks, value $3 each	9.00
One new stock, value $2.48	2.48
Theoretical value of four stocks	11.48

Theoretical ex-rights price = $2.87 ($11.48 ÷ 4).

The issue price of the new stocks, $2.48, is at a discount of $0.39 or 13.6% to the theoretical ex-rights price.

The discount has to be large enough to allow for the probable fall in the stock price on the announcement of the issue, but not so large as to raise concern about the financial health of the company.

Example
A specialist engineering company announced a four for five rights issue to raise $3 million. The main purpose of the funds was to acquire an engineering company. The new stocks were offered at $5 each. When the issue was announced the stock price was $6.70, but fell to $6.33 by the end of the day of the announcement.

Analysis
A four-for-five issue is a big issue for a company because the total number of the company's stocks will be increased by 80%. The company clearly believed that a large discount to the current stock price would be necessary. The actual discount to the stock price at the time of the announcement was $1.70 or about 25% ($1.70 ÷ $6.70). Not unusually, the stock price fell immediately on the announcement of the rights issue, in this case by 37¢ or over 5% by the end of the day.

New Stocks and Acquisitions

A company can acquire or merge with another company by issuing new stocks in exchange for the existing stocks of the other company.

Example

Alpha, a public company, has 200 million stocks in issue, currently priced at $3 per stock in the stock market. It has made an offer to buy 100% of the equity of Beta, a private company. Beta has 10 million stocks in issue, and the agreed value of Beta's stocks is $90 million.

Analysis

The valuation placed on Beta's stocks is $9 each ($90m ÷ 10m stocks). In a stock-for-stock acquisition Alpha would issue 30 million new stocks (valued at $90 million or $3 per stock). Beta stockholders would sell each of their stocks to Alpha in exchange for three Alpha stocks.

After the acquisition, Alpha's stock capital would consist of 230 million stocks and the assets of Alpha (that is the holding company for the group) would include an investment in 10 million Beta stocks, costing $90 million.

To make acquisitions by issuing new stocks in exchange for stocks in the target company, the company making the acquisitions ideally should have highly rated stocks, i.e. stocks with a high stock market price relative to the size of current profits and dividends. When this situation arises, there are more opportunities for attractive takeovers, to acquire subsidiaries whose stocks have a lower market rating.

Stock-for-stock (or paper) offers are not common in cross-border transactions, as a holding of stocks in an overseas company is not generally attractive to a target company's stockholders. In domestic transactions it is also very common for a full or partial cash alternative to be offered. Where this cannot be funded out of the bidding company's own cash resources it may be raised through an issue of stocks, underwritten by institutions that guarantee to take up sufficient stocks to fund as much of the cash alternative as is required.

Example

Gamma agrees to acquire 100% of the 50 million stocks of Delta at an agreed price of $4 per stock ($200 million in total). Gamma has offered two of its stocks (at an assumed value of $2 each) in exchange for every stock in Delta, or a cash alternative of $4. Gamma stocks are currently priced at $2.10, but the new issue has been underwritten at a price of $2.

Analysis
Gamma will acquire Delta's stocks by issuing 100 million of its own stocks. The stocks will either be issued to former Delta stockholders, or sold to underwriters at $2, to raise the cash to pay Delta stockholders who opt for the cash alternative.

Summary

Equity consists of common stock supplemented by retained profits and other reserves. Equity is a high-cost method of funding because, in the long term, equity holders will expect a higher return to compensate them for the risks of volatile earnings. However, companies must have a sufficient equity base to reassure lenders who want to avoid high exposure to credit risk.

Retained earnings are the major source of new equity, but companies might wish, or be obliged, to seek additional external funding from a new equity issue. The stock price and current stock market conditions can be critical when deciding whether and when to make such an issue.

Dividend policy affects the amount of profits that a company can retain to provide additional equity funding. In reality, however, cutting dividends to retain more profits could expose a company to the risk of a fall in its stock price. Dividend cuts should be a matter for caution, particularly when new equity funding might be required in the foreseeable future.

Debt

For most fairly large companies, the main options for debt financing are:

- bank facilities
- the bond market (only for companies with a single-A credit rating or better)
- private placements of debt securities (medium-term notes or commercial paper).

There are a number of issues to consider in deciding the precise form of debt capital structure and assembling a debt portfolio

- the maturity period (and debt profile)
- amortization
- interest rate basis (fixed or floating rate)
- currency of denomination (and currency swaps)
- source of finance (banks or capital markets)
- a term loan or a facility
- relative cost
- market conditions
- tax considerations
- covenants
- whether debt securities should be rated or unrated
- corporate resources and funding sources.

Maturity Period

Whereas equity funding is perpetual, (except in the rare cases where companies buy back and cancel some stocks) debt capital has a finite duration and must be repaid on or before maturity. A borrower has to decide the required term (maturity) for each new debt. For a major corporate borrower, debt can be of almost any duration. Walt Disney, the entertainment group, issued $300 million of bonds in July 1993 with a maturity of 100 years. Most companies, however, can arrange debt funding with maturities ranging from overnight up to ten years. The majority of companies are generally unable to raise funds for maturities over 10 years because lenders and investors are unwilling to accept the higher risk of default that is inevitable with longer-term debts.

Matched and Unmatched Funding

Debt funding can be either matched or unmatched.

- Matched funding occurs when the term of the debt matches the term of a project for which the funds are being raised.
- Unmatched funding occurs when the duration and maturity of the debt does not coincide with a funding requirement for a specific project.

As a general rule, funding for a major project should be matched, in order to be certain that funds would be available for the duration of the project and thereby avoid refinancing risk. Refinancing risk arises from the possibility that a borrower will be unable to obtain replacement funds (except at a high cost) when existing loans mature. This risk would occur if funding has to be renewed or extended during a project, because lenders might not be willing to provide new loans, perhaps because the financial prospects of the project or the company are less attractive and the perceived default risk has increased, or because conditions in the loan markets are less favorable to borrowers.

There are some situations in which a matched funding policy would be wholly inappropriate.

- Matched funding should be avoided when an excessive amount of debts would mature in the same year. Negotiating a refinancing package in these circumstances could be extremely onerous, or even impossible.

- In some debt markets, opportunities arise only occasionally to borrow at an attractive rate or for a particular maturity. These opportunities should be taken when available, because they might not be there when the funds are eventually needed.

With unmatched funding, a company raises money for a general funding pool, to cover its total requirements (based on its cash flow forecast), and does not borrow separately for each specific project. Funding activity broadly matches total funding requirements, and the company structures the maturity profile of the various debts in the funding pool to ensure that it will also have sufficient funds (or access to funds) to refinance or redeem its debts in an orderly and graduated way over a number of years. Managing the debt maturity profile is discussed in more detail in Chapter 8.

Amortization

Companies are often concerned about the schedule of principal repayments on bank loans that can affect their cash requirements. With amortizing loans, principal is repaid gradually over the term of the loan. In contrast with a bullet repayment, the loan is redeemed in full at maturity.

Interest Rate Basis – Fixed or Floating Rate

Funding can be arranged on either a fixed or a floating rate basis. With longer-term fixed rate funding, the rate of interest is set for the full term of the loan, by reference to the current yield on government bonds in the domestic bond markets. The interest rate will be the current yield on government bonds plus a spread to reflect the additional risk of default for lending to a corporation, rather than a lower-risk or, in some cases, risk-free domestic sovereign borrower. The size of the spread varies according to the perceived creditworthiness of the borrower and also the duration of the loan.

An investment grade company's cost of funds for a 10-year loan could be 100 basis points (100 bp or 1%) over the redemption yield of the reference (benchmark) government bond of similar maturity and 200bp (2%) or over for a 25-year loan. If the market price of the benchmark issue of 10-year government bonds gives investors a yield of 8% to redemption, a major company wishing to issue 10-year eurobonds would probably have to offer a yield of 9%, and perhaps more. Although long-term fixed-rate funding is readily available to larger companies, small and medium-sized companies (below a capitalization of $1 billion) are unlikely to obtain a fixed rate loan beyond three-to-five years' duration.

For floating-rate loans, the rate of interest is refined periodically (monthly, quarterly, bi-annually) by reference to the rate at which banks lend to each other for those periods, plus a margin.

For sterling, interbank lending rates are called the London Interbank Offered Rate (LIBOR). Each day, at 11.00am UK time, the quoted interbank lending rates are recorded for a number of major banks, and either an average rate or the rate quoted by one of those banks will be used as the benchmark (according to the terms of the loan agreement) for setting the interest rate on floating rate loans that fall due for refixing on that day.

The margin over LIBOR can be modest for high-quality companies, as low as 10bp (0.10%) or even less in some cases. For companies with a higher perceived risk of default, the margin can be as high as 500-700bp (5% to 7%) over LIBOR, or even higher in some cases.

In choosing between fixed and floating rate funding, there is a risk that the choice, in retrospect, will turn out to have been more expensive.

Example
A leisure, television and computer services group reported much improved profits under new management. A minor embarrassment for the group, however, was a decision some years earlier to lock in the cost of a portion of its debt at 12%. Following a subsequent sharp fall in interest rates, this decision in retrospect could be seen to have cost the

company substantially higher interest charges.

The choice between fixed- and floating-rate borrowing is made easier by the availability of interest rate swaps. A swap can be arranged

- by a company with a floating-rate debt, to exchange its floating-rate obligations for fixed-rate obligations, and
- by a company with fixed-rate debt, to exchange its fixed-rate obligations for floating-rate obligations.

In effect, a company can switch between fixed- and floating-rate borrowings at any time.

Example

Fiat, the Italian car-making group has, in recent years, preferred variable-rate borrowing to fixed- rate borrowing (particularly when the yield curve has been steep, with long-term borrowing rates much higher than short-term money market rates).

The company therefore has used swaps to

- switch from fixed-rate obligations (on bond issues) to variable-rate obligations (under a swap agreement), and in doing so
- reduced the cost of borrowing below the interest rate that the company would have had to pay by issuing variable-rate bonds, i.e. floating-rate notes or FRNs.

The group also has used some cross-currency swaps, issuing (fixed-rate) dollar bonds and swapping into (variable-rate) obligations in a European currency.

Whenever short-term interest rates are thought to have reached a low point, and are likely to start rising, i.e. the yield curve is expected to move from positive to flat or negative, companies are likely to want to fix the interest rate for medium-term debts. They can switch from variable rate to fixed-rate debt obligations by using interest rate swaps.

Currency of Denomination

Where possible, matched funding should be in the currency of the project being funded. For example, the purchase of a US company (a dollar-based asset) by a UK company ideally should be funded by dollar-denominated borrowings, so that the debt can be serviced by the dollar surpluses of the acquired business. By matching the currency of a liability (loan) with the currency of the assets that the loan is funding, exposures to currency risk will be minimized.

Example

A UK company purchases a US company for $6 million when the exchange rate is $1.50 = £1. The dollar earnings of the US subsidiary will cover loan repayments.

After six months, the exchange rate has changed to $1.60 = £1.

Analysis

To the UK company, the value of its investment in the US subsidiary at the time of the acquisition was £4 million ($6 million ÷ $1.50 to £1). The sterling value of the dollar loan was also £4 million. The sterling value is important because it is the currency in which the UK group will produce its consolidated accounts.

When the dollar subsequently weakens to $1.60, the sterling value of the US subsidiary becomes £3.75 million ($6 million ÷ $1.60 to £1). At the same time, the sterling value of the dollar loan has fallen to £3.75 million. The loss in the sterling value of the US subsidiary, due to the change in the dollar/sterling rate of exchange, is matched by the profit from a fall in the value of the loan.

Matching a dollar acquisition with a dollar loan thus provides a hedge against the risk of losses from adverse foreign exchange rate movements.

The relative absence of exchange controls for major currencies have made cross-border currency flows an everyday activity and made it easier to borrow in foreign currencies. The currency swap market also allows companies (and banks) to exchange a liability (or asset) in one currency for a liability (or asset) in another currency.

There are, however, some problems with foreign currency-denominated borrowing. In particular it can be difficult to obtain symmetrical tax treatment from the tax authorities for the profits and losses on foreign currency-denominated assets and the associated (hedging) loans.

As in all tax-related matters it is best to take expert advice before arranging foreign-currency-denominated borrowing, whether direct loans or currency swaps.

Source of Finance

Debt funding can be obtained either from banks or from investors in the capital markets, e.g. by issuing bonds. One difference between bank and non-bank finance is that non-bank investors require certainty of placement of their funds. The drawdown of the funds invariably takes place either at the outset of the loan, e.g. bond issue, or in a series of pre-arranged tranches. In contrast, banks often will provide funds on call in the form of a facility that might be drawn at any time.

Advantages of bank loans and facilities include

- the flexibility of the funding structure and the phased (amortized) repayment that can be negotiated, and
- the largely undisclosed nature of the funding. Bond issues, in contrast, are publicized both through the bond markets and the financial press.

A bank facility allows companies, in exchange for the payment of a commitment fee, to have funds available on demand if required. A committed bank facility is therefore a valuable resource because it avoids having to borrow (and incur interest charges) when the funds might be required for contingencies only.

Term Loan or Facility

It has been suggested in Chapter 2 that companies should arrange external funding needs into three categories:

- long-term (core) requirements
- short/medium-term cyclical requirements
- contingency requirements.

Having decided the proportion to be funded by new equity, debt or hybrid instruments; companies then have to consider how the debt element of planned funding should be structured, as a mixture of term loans and committed facilities.

A committed facility is an arrangement for a specific term (most commonly five years) in which the bank agrees to provide funds at the request of the customer, at a pre-arranged margin over the interest rates prevailing at the time of drawdown. In return the bank levies a pre-arranged commitment fee (payable periodically).

A bank facility allows companies, in exchange for the payment of a commitment fee, to have funds available on demand if required. A committed bank facility is therefore a valuable resource because it avoids having to borrow (and incur interest charges) when the funds might be required for contingencies only.

With a term loan, the funds are received in full at the outset, and any money that is surplus to immediate requirements will be reinvested, probably at a yield lower than the interest cost on the funds. Therefore a facility should be cheaper if the company's requirements for the funds are cyclical, or build up over time.

Relative Cost

The relative cost of different types of debt is a major factor in borrowing decisions. The cost of debt fluctuates, both as a result of general economic or market conditions, and also as a result of factors specific to a particular market. For example, the cost of a bank facility for an investment grade-rated company can be very cheap, particularly as banking becomes more global, mainly for two reasons:

- the intensity of competition between banks for lending business
- an expectation by banks that they would be able to cross-sell other banking products to major corporate customers, having won their loan business.

Example

A major company arranged a Multiple Option Facility (MOF), a syndicated bank loan facility, at a commitment fee of just four basis points (0.04%) per annum and a drawing margin of just 7.5 basis points over LIBOR. In contrast, prices in the loans market in the 1990s were much higher. A combination of factors, such as the economic recession and its effect on company profits, the weak financial position of many banks, and tighter capital adequacy requirements that were being applied to banks, led to a sharp increase in the cost of facilities. The comparative cost of a facility for the same company in 1998 was a commitment fee of approximately 20 basis points and a drawing margin of 50 basis points over LIBOR.

A company should try to obtain funds at the lowest available cost. Trying to obtain funds cheaply calls for judgment about when to borrow, as well as where to borrow. Interest rates change, and there is, of course, always the risk that in retrospect a different funding arrangement would have been cheaper.

- A bank loan might be arranged at a floating rate of interest. If interest rates subsequently go up, a fixed-rate loan would probably have been cheaper.
- A company might borrow at a fixed rate in the bond markets or from a bank just before there is a fall in the general level of interest rates.
- A UK company might arrange a US dollar loan to finance UK operations if interest rates were lower in the US than in the UK. If the dollar subsequently rose in value against sterling, the cost of

servicing the loan out of UK earnings would become more expensive. The benefit of a low interest rate would be offset by the cost of the unfavorable movement in the dollar/sterling exchange rate.

It is usually necessary for a chief operating officer or treasurer to estimate what the cost of a particular debt option might be. For example, suppose that a company is considering a eurobond issue at a fixed coupon rate of interest. A bank wishing to lead-manage the issue might advise that the bond could be issued at a price that would give investors a yield of 170 basis points over a specified benchmark interest rate, i.e. the yield on a benchmark issue of government bonds with the same maturity.

Two factors would make the actual interest cost uncertain until the issue takes place:

- changes in market interest rates, that would cause a rise or fall in the yield on the benchmark bond, and
- the ability of the lead manager to price the issue at the expected yield of 170 basis points above this benchmark rates.

When the bond issue is planned, the benchmark government bond rate might have been 7.5% and the company therefore would expect to price its bond issue to yield 9.2% (7.5% plus 170bp). If, however, by the date of the company's bond issue, the yield on the benchmark bond has risen to 7.7%, and the bonds are priced at a spread of 180 basis points over this rate, the actual yield, i.e. the cost to the company, would be 9.5% (7.7% plus 180bp).

Market Conditions

Funds are not always available from some sources. This is particularly the case in some capital markets where the secondary market sometimes can be illiquid.

Smaller companies cannot access some markets. Medium-sized companies, for example, would find it costly to raise funds in foreign domestic markets.

Many markets are window markets, in which the relative cost of funds fluctuates regularly, according to the weight of funding activity and the liquidity of the market at any time.

Funding rates were particularly volatile in many markets in the turbulent financial periods of 1998.

One example of the impact of market conditions on debt finance is shown below.

Example
August 1998 saw the biggest corporate bond sale ever, by WorldCom Inc. to finance its acquisition of MCI Communications Corporation. WorldCom issued 46 billion in bonds in four tranches, with spreads over Treasuries as follows:

> $1.5 billion three-year notes at 70 bp
> $500 million of five-year notes at 83 bp
> $2.25 billion of seven-year notes at 94 bp
> $1.5 billion of 30-year bonds at 135 bp.

The offer was increased by 20% after investors' initial orders exceeded the bonds available for sale.

Tax Considerations and Offshore Financial Centers

The taxation implications of borrowing (particularly for multinational companies borrowing in a variety of different currencies) can affect the funding decision. What may appear to be the cheapest pre-tax borrowing method is not necessarily the case, once tax concessions are considered.

Multinational companies often establish a specialist finance company in an offshore financial center and use the finance company to raise debt capital.

Offshore financial centers, that also are commonly known as tax havens, have three characteristics:

- they operate low-tax or nil-tax regimes
- they are lightly regulated
- they specialize in doing business with non-resident companies and/or individuals.

The purpose of locating a finance company in a tax haven is to maximize the value of interest deductions. The finance company can raise capital and re-lend the money to other companies within the group. By ensuring careful tax planning, the after-tax costs of raising capital can be reduced significantly.

Tax legislation varies between countries and states, and often can be quite complex.

When a finance company within a multinational group acts as fund-raiser for the rest of the group, lenders will require guarantees from the holding company, and possibly from other companies in the group. Guarantees mean that investors, e.g. bondholders, are in effect lending to the group as a whole, and can assess the credit risk accordingly.

Refinancing Using an Offshore Finance Company

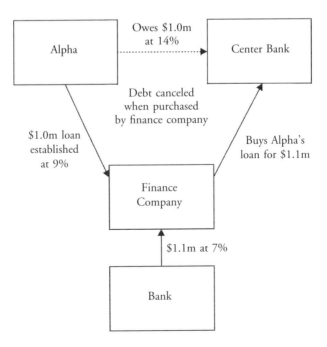

Covenants

Covenants are undertakings given by a borrower to a lender for the duration of a loan agreement. While covenants can differ between one loan agreement and another, typical covenants include an agreement by the borrower that

- it will not pledge its assets to another lender, i.e. will not create a class of creditor that ranks above the lender in the hierarchy of creditors (a negative pledge covenant)
- its gearing ratio will not fall below a stipulated minimum level
- the ratio of its annual profits before interest to interest costs (interest cover) will not fall below a stipulated minimum
- it will not dispose of significant assets during the term of the loan.

A breach of covenant constitutes an event of default, giving the lender (or trustees for the lenders) the right to take action against the borrower.

Covenant requirements have become more onerous in recent years, in view of the high levels of company failures in the economic recession of the early 1990s. A company wishing to borrow should therefore consider the nature and extent of the covenants on different types of borrowing. Covenant requirements vary according to the type of loan or debt.

The most restrictive covenants are applied by banks to their loans. The bond, MTN and CP markets, however, also have begun to apply tougher covenants.

As a general rule, covenants are more exacting for loans or bond issues with a longer maturity. Clearly, a company must make concessions if it wishes to borrow money, and must agree to certain covenants. However, there is room to negotiate the precise form and nature of the covenants, regardless of a company's size.

A company should not overlook the potential consequences of obtaining loans by agreeing to onerous covenants. Covenants become significant only when a company gets into financial difficulties and is therefore desperate for either new or continued funding.

Breach of Covenants

A potential breach of covenants can force a company to renegotiate its debts with banks. By anticipating a breach, and seeking an early remedy, a company can avoid aggravating its financial difficulties.

Example
EuroDisney, operator of Europe's largest theme park, was originally financed in 1989 by an equity issue and substantial debt. The park was opened in 1992 but two years later, in the face of escalating financial costs and lower-than-expected earnings, its lenders were obliged to suspend debt and lease payments to allow the park to stay open. The agreement was for repayments and interest to be phased in from fiscal 1998. Despite the reprieve from closure, the company's stocks fell from an issue price of 72 francs in 1989, to a December 1998 level of 8.25 francs in expectation of losses once the loan agreement expired.

Rated or Unrated Debt

Rated debt is any capital markets debt issue that carries a credit rating from one or more rating agencies. These agencies are independent credit assessment services, the two best-known being Moody's Investors Services and Standard & Poor's. A credit rating is optional, and a company must ask an agency to provide a rating for a debt issue. A credit rating provides an independent and reliable assessment of the credit risk for holders of the debt securities. This can influence the interest rate on the debt, and also how restrictive the covenants must be to satisfy investors. Rated debt is normally cheaper than unrated debt bearing the same perceived credit risk, although the cost of rate debt depends on the quality of the rating.

In some markets such as the US commercial paper market (USCP) and the Japanese public market, a rating is essential. Without it, investors would not buy the company's debt. In other markets, such as the eurocommercial paper (ECP) market, a borrower can choose whether or not to obtain a rating.

In theory, ratings are available to all public companies with a five-year track record. In practice, however, the cost of obtaining a rating, and of maintaining a rating are high, and a company can probably justify a rating only if it plans to borrow at least $100 million in markets where credit ratings will affect the cost of borrowing.

Credit ratings of the two principal rating agencies, Moody's and Standard & Poor's, in descending order of creditworthiness, are shown on the opposite page.

The rating for a debt issue, e.g. a bond issue or commercial paper issue, is monitored regularly. In the event of an improvement or a deterioration in the perceived strength of the company, the rating agencies will either upgrade or downrate the rating, as appropriate.

Credit Ratings and Borrowing Costs

A credit rating is a measure of perceived credit risk, so the interest rate at which investors are prepared to lend to a company varies according to the rating. The difference in cost might be just a few basis points between, say, an A1+ and an A1 rating. However, the difference can be much greater for a company with a lower rating. Many banks and institutions, particularly in the US and Japan, restrict their lending activity to high-rated companies, e.g. to companies whose existing debt issues are in the investment grade category. When a company's debt is downgraded from investment grade to non-investment grade, it can be difficult, perhaps impossible, for the company to obtain new funds.

For example, suppose a company obtains an A2/A rating for a bond issue, and the rating is subsequently downgraded to say Baa1/BBB+. The downgrading could influence potential bond investors more than if the rating had never been achieved (as a consequence of the public announcement of the downrating). Some major companies that would command investment-grade ratings have therefore opted to remain unrated and confine themselves to those markets where ratings are not essential even if they have to pay more for their funds.

Ratings for Short-Term Debt

	Moody's	Standard & Poor's
Investment grade rating	P1 P2 B3	A1 A2 A3
Speculative grade	Not Prime	B, C

Ratings for Long-Term Debt

	Moody's	Standard & Poor's	Comment
	Aaa1 Aaa2 Aaa3	AAA+ AAA AAA-	Best quality bonds
	Aa1 Aa2 Aa3	AA+ AA AA-	Very strong capacity to pay interest and repay principal
	A1 A2 A3	A+ A A-	Strong capacity to pay interest and repay principal
Investment grade rating	Baa1 Baa2 Baa3	BBB+ BBB BBB-	Payment capacity is adequate. Adverse business conditions could make payment capacity inadequate
	Ba1 Ba2 Ba3	BB+ BB BB-	Speculative grade investment. Future cannot be assured. Moderate protection for interest and principal payments
	B	B	Highly vulnerable to adverse business conditions
	Caa Ca	CCC CC	Identifiable vulnerability to default

Corporate Resources and Funding Sources

The resources available to a company for arranging loans and facilities are largely dependent on the scale of its activities. Companies that borrow regularly and in large quantities will have a larger treasury department, and a wider network of financial advisers and contacts in the banking community and the capital markets. With larger-scale resources, a company is able to consider a wider range of borrowing options.

Logistical Difficulties

The difficulties of organizing fund-raising activities can deter even major corporations from borrowing in certain markets. For example, a US company might be deterred from borrowing in yen in the domestic private placement markets of Japan because of administrative and arrangement problems in the Japanese markets.

Hybrid Financial Instruments

Hybrid financial instruments are securities issued by a company that combine features of both equity and debt. Typically, they offer investors

- a fixed income for several years, and
- the opportunity to acquire equity stocks in the company, on or after a specified future date.

Types of Hybrid Instrument

The most common types of hybrid instrument are:

- convertible bonds
- convertible preferred stocks*
- bonds with equity warrants attached.

*Straight preferred stocks also can be regarded as a form of hybrid instrument because they have characteristics that are comparable partly with those of equity stocks and partly with those of debt capital.

Convertible Bonds

Convertible bonds are unsecured fixed-interest bonds that give their holders the right, at some future date, to convert the bonds into equity stocks of the company, at a fixed rate of conversion. If the bonds are not converted into equity, they must be redeemed on or before maturity by the issuer.

The coupon interest rate, that is fixed, is usually lower than the coupon that would have to be paid on a similar issue of straight bonds, issued at the same time and for the same maturity. This is because investors in convertibles are prepared to accept a lower interest yield in return for the option to convert the bonds into equity at a future date.

One of the attractions of convertible bonds to investors is that if the share price rises sufficiently over time, there will be an opportunity to profit from converting the bonds into equity.

Convertible bonds can have a variety of other features.

- Zero-coupon convertibles, fairly common in the US, pay no interest to bondholders up to their maturity/conversion date. However, they are issued at a deep discount to their nominal value (par), and are redeemable at par.
- A convertible could be issued with a call option, giving the issuer (the company) the right to insist on redemption of the bonds before maturity. When an issuer exercises a call option, bondholders have a short period of time in which to convert the bonds into stocks, should they wish.
- Some convertible bonds have been issued with put options, giving bondholders the right to insist that the issuer should redeem the bonds (usually at a premium to par value) before maturity. Some issues of convertibles have offered put options on terms that make it almost certain that the options will be exercised, and the bonds redeemed before maturity.

Preferred Stock

Preferred stocks are non-equity stocks. Depending on their features, they can be considered a form of funding that is neither equity nor debt, but lies somewhere between the two.

- They give their holders the right to receive an annual dividend, but only up to a specified limit. The dividend is commonly a fixed amount expressed as a percentage (coupon rate) of the face value of the stocks.
- They rank ahead of common stockholders in the event of a liquidation of the company, but behind creditors.

- Preferred stocks can be redeemable or non-redeemable, i.e. permanent.

Convertible Preferred Stocks

Convertible preferred stocks, unlike straight preferred stocks, give their holders the right but not the obligation to convert their stockholding into equity on or after a specified date, at a fixed rate of exchange. Usually they are redeemable if not converted, and are therefore similar to convertible bonds.

Equity Warrant Bonds

Equity warrant bonds are bonds issued with equity warrants attached. Warrants are similar to share options, and give their holder the right but not the obligation to subscribe for a fixed quantity of equity stocks in the company at a future date, and at a fixed subscription price (exercise price).

When bonds are issued with warrants, the warrants are detachable and can be sold in the stock market separately from the bonds. Investors might therefore subscribe to an issue of equity warrant bonds, hold the bonds to maturity (as a long-term investment) and sell the warrants in the stock market fairly soon after purchase.

Equity warrant bonds are unsecured, and offer a lower coupon rate of interest than similar straight bonds issued at the same time and for the same maturity. In these respects, they are similar to convertible bonds.

A feature of equity warrant bonds is that if the warrants are exercised, the money obtained from issuing the new stocks can be used to help redeem the bonds. The debt capital (the bonds) therefore will be replaced, in part at least, by new equity.

Equity warrant bonds were used extensively in 1988-89 by Japanese companies to raise capital in the euroconvertibles market. Most had a five-year term, with the warrants exercisable at maturity of the bonds. Following the start of the collapse in Japanese share prices in 1989, the warrants linked to the bond issues became worthless because they had an exercise price well above the current share price.

When some of these equity warrant bond issues matured in the mid-1990s, cash had to be found to redeem the bonds. Because share prices were then quite low, some of the companies were able to issue new equity warrant bonds. The cash from the new bond issues was used to redeem the maturing debt.

Since the collapse of the late 1980s, equity warrant bonds have not regained their popularity. In the late 1990s they have had limited, specialist appeal, notably in Germany and Switzerland.

Exchangeable stocks

Another development specific to the late 1990s is the rise of the exchangeables market. These are bonds that the issuer redeems in another company's stocks, often allowing it to divest non-core stockholdings. In France and Japan, for instance, a large proportion of stocks in companies is held by other companies, rather than by insurance or pension funds.

Derivatives can be a better way of rationalizing such corporate cross-holdings than selling them in the market. For example, in February 1998 when telecoms company Bell Atlantic merged with Nynex, it was prevented under the terms of the merger agreement from selling a significant holding for two years; this problem was solved by the issue of a $2.45 billion bond, exchangeable for its stake in Telecom New Zealand in April 2003.

Later, in April 1998, Swiss Life Finance issued $2 billion of equity-linked bonds in six separate tranches, exchangeable into stocks in Glaxo-Wellcome, Mannesmann, Royal Dutch/Shell, Unilever, Novartis and UBS, all of which were part of Swiss Life's equity portfolio.

The rise of the exchangeables market is illustrative of how the highly flexible hybrid instrument market can respond to specific funding needs.

Advantages of Hybrid Funding

The total volume of hybrid funding by companies is small relative to the amount of equity or debt capital. There could be circumstances, however, when companies might benefit from hybrid funding.

Convertibles (bonds or preferred stocks) and equity warrant bonds can be issued with a lower coupon rate of interest than similar straight debt. Investors are willing to accept a lower interest yield in return for the prospect of capital gains from converting the bonds into equity.

Example
In February 1998 Parmalat, the Italian food and drink company, launched the first euro-denominated corporate convertible bond. Unusually this issue included a step-down premium whereby the premium would be reduced from 34% in years one to six to 26% in years seven to eight, to encourage investors to wait until year six before converting. The deal attracted an enormous amount of interest and sold out within the hour because of investors' enthusiasm for euro-denominated paper.

Interest on convertible bonds and equity warrant bonds is usually an allowable charge for tax purposes, so that their after-tax cost to the company is lower than the gross yield to investors. Dividends on preferred stocks, on the other hand, are not an allowable expense for tax purposes. An advantage of preferred stocks over bonds, however, from the issuer's point of view, is that non-payment of a preferred dividend would not breach a loan agreement.

In terms of planning a company's capital structure, hybrids

- increase financial gearing in the short term, but
- create the possibility of lower gearing in the future, if and when conversion into equity takes place.

Hybrid instruments need to attract investors, as well as offer benefits to the issuer. Investors might be willing to buy convertibles or equity warrant bonds because they are attracted by the limited downside risk and by the opportunity to benefit from the upside potential of a rising share price.

- The fixed dividend or coupon, with a prior right of payment ahead of equity dividends, gives investors the security of a regular income, i.e. lower risk than equity.
- Hybrids, therefore, offer the reassuring comfort of a regular return on capital investment.
- Investors stand to benefit by converting into equity in the event that the company's share price rises sufficiently over time.

In a falling stock market, the fixed interest or dividend payments limit the fall in the market price of convertibles, whereas in a rising market the price of convertibles rises broadly in line with the price of equity.

Earnings per Share and Deferred Equity

One possible advantage of hybrid funding is that the company's earnings per share can be protected in the short term, i.e. in the period up to conversion. In contrast, by issuing new equity immediately, there could be some dilution in earnings per share.

Suppose, for example, that a company needs long-term funds to finance a new project. Annual profits from the project will build up over some years, but will be quite small in the early years. If the company wants to finance the project in the long term with equity, it could opt for an issue of convertible bonds (or possibly preferred stocks), because in the short term the cost of interest on the convertibles probably will be lower than the cost of the dividends that equity stockholders would expect.

Example
Alpha, a public company, wishes to raise $100 million to finance a new project. Returns from the project in the first five years, before tax, are expected to be:

Year	Income before interest and tax
	$ million
1	7
2	7
3	8
4	8
5	10

The project could be financed by a new equity issue. Stockholders in Alpha will require a 5% return on the value of their stocks, and dividend growth of 5% per annum.

Alternatively, the project could be financed by an issue of $100 million of 7% convertible bonds. These would be convertible into equity after four years. Interest on the bonds would be allowable for tax at 30%.

Summary

Hybrid funding is used in a variety of circumstances:

- to take advantage of a lower coupon rate of interest than on straight debt
- to raise long-term capital, but defer the creation of new equity to avoid a short-term dilution in earnings per share
- to increase the company's equity base when the markets are more receptive to a bond issue than a new issue of equity
- in leveraged transactions, particularly where a major provider of funds is a venture capital institution.

There is one significant disadvantage to hybrid funding. Company management might regard equity conversion at some time in the future as a certainty rather than a possibility. For conventional convertible issues, the conversion price is usually between 10% and 25% above the prevailing share price at the time of issue and conversion is several years away. It might therefore seem likely that the share price will rise sufficiently to make conversion a profitable option for the bondholders. However, if the share price does not rise sufficiently, and conversion does not occur, the company will have to obtain new funds to redeem the maturing convertible bond.

Convertibles are often issued by high-growth, highly leveraged companies, and if these are short of cash, raising new loans to redeem maturing loans can be a problem. This is an example of refinancing risk. This problem is particularly severe when the company is going through difficult times, commercially and financially, because there will be a struggle to obtain new finance. For example, the financial problems of Saatchi & Saatchi, the advertising agency group, in the mid-1990s, were compounded by a convertible bond issue approaching the date when bondholders could exercise put options and call for a redemption of their bonds.

7

Optimal Capital Structure

The optimal capital structure for a company should be the mix of equity, debt and hybrid instruments that minimizes the overall cost of funding, i.e. it should minimize the company's weighted average cost of capital. In practice, however, it is not possible to specify this optimal capital structure exactly, for any individual company.

It clearly makes sense to obtain funds at the lowest possible cost. In the long run, debt is cheaper than equity. However, when a company's financial leverage increases as it takes on more debt capital, there is an increasing risk for stockholders. The cost of equity therefore will rise, perhaps offsetting the benefits of raising cheap debt capital.

Although management cannot be specific about the optimal capital structure for their company, they should at least be aware of

- how banks and the capital markets might respond to an increase in the company's leverage level if it were to borrow new funds, and
- whether the company is sufficiently low geared to make new debt capital an attractive option, compared to a new issue of equity as a fund-raising measure.

Reactive and Proactive Approaches

There are two approaches to managing a company's capital structure: a reactive and a proactive approach.

The reactive approach is to take funding decisions when a requirement for more – or less – funding becomes apparent, and to raise or reduce capital by the method that seems best at the time.

The proactive approach, that is found in companies with large and well-organized treasury functions, is to

- forecast future funding requirements or funding surpluses as much as possible
- establish targets for capital structure, in particular a target leverage level (a target range) and a target maturity profile for debt capital
- if appropriate, raise funds early when new funding requirements are anticipated, in order to take advantage of favorable conditions in the capital markets or low bank lending rates.

This approach calls for accurate and flexible forecasting skills, and good treasury management systems.

A proactive approach also can be taken to reducing funds, whenever a company considers its current funding to be in excess of requirements for the foreseeable, long-term future. By having a target leverage level and a target debt maturity profile, management can decide which method of removing surplus capital might be more appropriate, i.e.

- reducing equity, by raising dividends or buying back and canceling stocks, or
- redeeming loans early.

Example
Delta, a public company, has net assets of $1 billion that are financed by equity and medium-term or long-term debt, in the ratio 70%:30%. The company's management has set a target for leverage. Measuring leverage as the ratio of medium-term or long-term debt to equity, the company's target leverage level should be kept in the range 33.3% to 100%. At a leverage level of 100%, debt capital would equal equity capital in value.

The company's business plan for the next three years, allowing for future profits and dividend policy, includes the following estimates:

	Capital Requirements in total (by year-end)	Retained earnings for the year
	$ million	$ million
Now	1,000	-
Year 1	1,500	100
Year 2	2,000	200
Year 3	2,500	300

No existing debts will mature during this period.

Delta's management has ambitious growth plans for the company, and wishes to decide how the future funding requirements of the company should be met.

Analysis
The maximum debt capital the company should have, given its targets for leverage, is as follows:

Total capital required	Maximum debt (50%)
$m	$m
1,000	500
1,500	750
2,000	1,000
2,500	1,250

Approach 1
There are many ways of funding the company within the target leverage level. A useful starting point, however, might be to assess whether the company could meet its funding requirements, and remain within its target leverage level, by relying entirely on retained earnings and extra debt capital.

	Total capital required	Equity at start of year	Retained earnings	Equity at end of year	*Debt	Leverage ratio
	$m	$m	$m	$m	$m	%
Year 1	1,500	700	100	800	700	87.5
Year 2	2,000	800	200	1,000	1,000	100.0
Year 3	2,500	1,000	300	1,300	1,200	92.3

* balance to make up capital requirement

The company could just remain within its maximum target leverage level, by relying on retained earnings and new debt. This would call for new debt capital of $900 million over the three-year period, as follows:

	Total new capital raised		New equity (retained earnings)	New debt	
	$m		$m	$m	
Year 1	500	(1,500 - 1,000)	100	400	(700 - 300)
Year 2	500	(2,000 - 1,500)	200	300	(1,000 - 700)
Year 3	500	(2,500 - 2,000)	300	200	(1,200 - 1,000)
Total	1,500		600	900	

If the company's forecast of retained earnings were too optimistic, the company would need to make up the shortfall in its funding requirements by raising new equity, otherwise its leverage level would become too high.

Approach 2

An alternative plan for Delta that also should be considered is the minimum amount of new debt required to remain within the leverage target. The company's management believes firmly that Delta's leverage should not fall below 33.3%. This is a ratio of debt to equity of 1:3, suggesting that debt capital should make up at least one-quarter of the company's funds.

	Total capital	Minimum debt	Actual debt
	$m	$m	$m
Now	1,000	250	300
Year 1	1,500	375	
Year 2	2,000	500	
Year 3	2,500	625	

This suggests that the company should raise extra debt capital of at least $325 million over three years ($625m - $300m). There should be extra debt of at least $75 million in Year 1 ($375m - $300m) a further $125 million by Year 2 ($500m - $375m) and a further $125 million by Year 3 ($625m - $500m). With a further $600 million expected from retained earnings over the three-year period, the remaining funding deficit to be financed by either new equity or new debt is as follows:

	Total funding	New funding	Retained earnings	Minimum new debt	Balance (new equity or debt)	
	$m	$m	$m	$m	$m	
Now	1,000	-	-	-	-	
Year 1	1,500	500	100	75	325	(500 - 100 - 75)
Year 2	2,000	500	200	125	175	(500 - 200 - 125)
Year 3	2,500	500	300	125	75	(500 - 300 - 125)

Delta's management can make funding decisions, based on the business plan and within the target range for leverage, by selecting new equity or new debt (within the planned limits) according to conditions in the capital markets and loan market, and according to their preferred for higher or lower leverage.

Variations in Capital Structure over Time

Inevitably, a company's capital structure is never static and will change over time. Retained earnings that should be earned continually add to equity and reduce leverage levels. It is not unusual, therefore, for companies to experience funding cycles of high leverage, as new loans are obtained to fund capital expansion, and

decreasing leverage, as retained earnings are earned. The cash flows generated from profits could be used to redeem loans and thereby replace debt capital with equity in the company's capital structure.

Example
Gamma, a public company with a stock market listing, has pursued a policy in recent years of raising capital, when required, through borrowing at the lowest rate available when the funds are needed. Maturing loans are either refinanced or repaid from the cash flows from retained earnings. The capital funding profile over the past four to five years has been as follows:

	Year 1	Year 2	Year 3	Year 4	Year 5
	$m	$m	$m	$m	$m
Equity at start of year	1,600	1,600	1,800	2,100	2,400
Debt at start of year	1,200	1,900	2,200	1,900	1,600
Total funds at start of year	2,800	3,500	4,000	4,000	4,000
Retained earnings in the year	0	200	300	300	
Debt redeemed during the year	(200)	(100)	(300)	(300)	
New debt obtained in the year	900	400	0	0	
Net change in debt	+700	+300	(300)	(300)	

Analysis
The changing capital structure of the company is shown clearly in the diagram overleaf.

The table and diagram show that the company has used debt capital to meet all new external funding requirements when retained earnings are insufficient. Over time, leverage increases as funding requirements rise and more debt capital is obtained to meet them. Eventually, however, the company is able to reduce leverage by replacing maturing debts with new equity capital in the form of retained earnings.

Illustrative gearing/funding mix over time

$000m

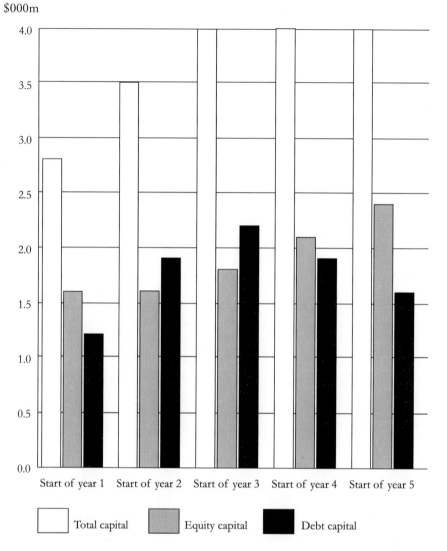

| Total capital | Equity capital | Debt capital |

Leverage and Financial Risk

It is important to understand the link between leverage and financial risk.

High leverage creates financial risks for a company in two ways.

- A company must meet its debt payment obligations otherwise its loan creditors could expose it to action. When debt obligations are high, profits must be sufficient to cover them.
- Profits available to stockholders, after paying debt interest, can fluctuate sharply from one year to the next. The risk for stockholders therefore can be very high. A change in profits (before interest) of a given percentage amount will result in a bigger percentage change in profits (after interest and tax) for stockholders. This percentage change will be larger for more highly geared companies.

Example 1

Two companies, Echo and Foxtrot, are identical in every respect except for their leverage. Echo has no debt capital, and Foxtrot is financed 50% by debt and 50% by equity. The interest cost of Foxtrot's debt is 10% per annum. Details about each of the companies in the year just ended are as follows:

	Echo	Foxtrot
	$m	$m
Equity	10	5
Debt	=	5
Total capital	10	10
	$000	$000
Earnings before interest and tax	1,000	1,000
Interest	0	500
Earnings before tax	1,000	500
Tax (30%)	300	150
Dividends for stockholders	700	350
Earnings per $1 of equity	$\frac{\$700{,}000}{10\text{ million}} = \$0.07$	$\frac{\$350{,}000}{5\text{ million}} = \$0.07$

To simplify the example, it is assumed that all profits for stockholders are distributed as dividends.

Analysis

Suppose that profits before interest fall next year by 10%, from $1 million to $900,000. The effect on each company will be as follows:

	Echo	Foxtrot
	$000	$000
Income before interest and tax	900	900
Interest	0	500
Income before tax	900	400
Tax (30%)	270	120
Dividends for stockholders	630	280
Income per $1 of equity	$\frac{\$630,000}{10 \text{ million}} = \$0.063$	$\frac{\$280,000}{5 \text{ million}} = \$0.056$

Dividends for stockholders have fallen by 10% in Echo, an unleveraged company, in response to a 10% fall in trading profits. In contrast, profits for stockholders in Foxtrot, a fairly highly leveraged company, have fallen by a bigger percentage amount. The fall in Foxtrot's profits per stock – in this example, the fall in profit per $1 of equity – is 20%, from $0.07 to $0.056.

Just as earnings per stock will fall more rapidly in a leveraged company when profits fall, earnings per stock also will rise more rapidly when profits climb. Stockholders seeking a high return could be attracted to highly leveraged companies, despite the potential risk that profits might not rise as expected.

Setting a Suitable Target Leverage Level

When management opts for a proactive approach to capital structuring, it could decide to set a target range for the company's leverage ratio.

The leverage target should balance the conflicting requirements of stockholders who require a high return on their equity together with tolerable risk. The risk-return balance varies from company to company, and over time for the same company. A property development company normally would be more highly geared than a manufacturing company, for example, because equity investors in a property development company usually are looking to add a higher risk-higher return dimension to their investment portfolio.

A start-up company backed by venture capital typically will have a ratio of debt to equity of between 1:1 and 5:1. The same company, as it develops successfully, will reduce its leverage level over time, perhaps to a debt:equity ratio of about 1:2. Having quantified a target leverage level, management should convert the target into planned actions. This planning process should involve the operating departments as well as the company's treasury department.

For example, operating managers can plan to improve efficiency in stockholding and control work-in-progress levels. By controlling working capital more efficiently, long-term funding requirements will be reduced, creating scope to reduce the leverage level.

A commonly quoted leverage target for major industrial companies is 40%, meaning $4 of debt for every $10 of equity, i.e. $4 of debt for every $14 of capital. This target, however, has no particular scientific basis and is inappropriate for many companies. A target leverage level should simply represent a level of debt that should not threaten the company's financial position.

Conclusion

For companies with large or variable funding requirements, a proactive approach to leverage policy is highly desirable, and a target range should be set for the leverage level, and for the debt maturity profile that is discussed in the next chapter. Managing the leverage level should not be the main driving force behind business activity. Nevertheless, managers need to be aware of the implications of leverage and capital requirements for their companies' longer-term development strategy.

Leverage affects how much a company can afford to invest in further organic or acquisitive growth. Leverage decisions therefore can have important repercussions for non-financial managers who will wish to develop their part of the business. Because setting a leverage target calls for an assessment of commercial risks and operating efficiency, as well as taking a view on financial risk and earnings volatility, it is appropriate to involve non-financial managers in the target-setting process.

Debt Profile Management

8

Although a company's non-financial managers should be involved in setting the target leverage level and implementing action that moves the company towards this target level, it is the responsibility of the finance director or treasurer to raise the external funds required for refinancing and growth.

The leverage target should guide the choice between equity, debt and hybrid funding. For the debt capital requirements, management also should decide on the most appropriate debt profile (or debt portfolio).

What is a Debt Profile?

A debt profile or debt portfolio is the mixture of different types of debt capital in a company's total debt. For example:

- debt maturing at different times (in different years)
- bank loans, bank facilities, commercial paper programs, bonds, etc.
- debt in domestic currency and foreign currencies.

Debt Maturity Profile

A company should try to ensure that its debt structure has a graduated maturity profile, with debts scheduled to mature at different times.

When the debt profile shows a spread of debts maturing over a number of years, the company should be able to

- arrange an orderly refinancing program (to replace maturing debt), or
- make sure that sufficient cash is available from other sources to retire the debts as they mature.

In contrast, if a company is faced with the redemption of a large proportion of its debts within a short space of time, the refinancing risk could be high. Without cash from other sources to repay the maturing debt, the company would be forced to enter refinancing negotiations with its bankers in order to raise new funds to meet its repayment obligations. Refinancing agreements are considered in more detail in Chapter 9.

Constructing a Maturity Profile

A debt profile can be constructed showing

- how much debt finance the company has in place (a distinction can be made between utilized funds and unutilized facilities), and
- when the debt will mature.

An illustrative debt maturity profile is shown overleaf. This analyzes a company's existing debts and bank facilities, and is quite typical of the profile that might be expected of a large commercial company.

Using a Debt Profile

The debt profile can be compared with planned funding requirements to establish what new borrowing will be needed over the next few years, either to replace maturing loans or to fund future business growth.

The profile also can be used to manage the tiering of the company's debts, to ensure that an excessive quantity of loans does not mature at the same time. For each year (or time band) estimates should be made for:

Illustrative debt maturity profile

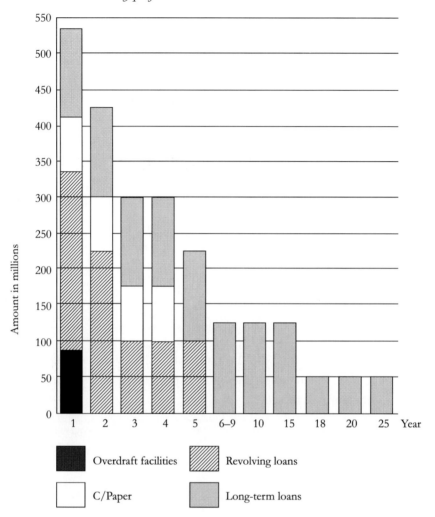

The total external funds required for planned activities		A
New equity		B
New debt funding for planned activities		A - B
Debt funding or facilities for contingencies		C
Total debt funding required		A - B + C

Management should examine the various debt-funding options available in each band to meet funding requirements. For a large multinational company, these are broadly as follows. (For smaller companies, some of these funding options are inappropriate or unavailable.)

Time band	Source	Debt funding options
0-5 years	Banks	Bilateral bank facility Syndicated bank facility Term loan
	Capital markets	Eurocommercial paper (ECP) US commercial paper (issues of USCP must be backed by committed bank facilities) Other commercial paper, e.g. sterling CP, Canadian CP, etc. Eurobond market (short-dated bonds) US private placement market
5-10 years	Banks	Term loan
	Capital markets	Eurobond market US public or private markets German private placement market (Schuldscheine) US/European medium-term note market Japanese private placement market Tax-based schemes Hybrid finance (convertibles, etc.)

Continual Review

Financial management should review the debt profile/portfolio of the company regularly, at least once a year, against the business plan cash forecast. Target funding projections should be updated to allow for any change in business projections. The target leverage structure, debt requirements, and debt profile should be reconsidered and amended if appropriate in the light of any changes since the last review.

Active Debt Management

Some large companies with well-organized treasury departments are willing to use the company's debt-raising capability to improve profits. This can be called active debt management.

A key feature of this approach is a willingness to borrow and a continual search for opportunities to borrow cheaply. The low-cost funds then can be redeployed to improve profits, with little or no additional risk.

Active debt management requires:

- constant monitoring of the company's cash needs, funding capability and conditions in the loan markets, money markets and capital markets
- flexibility in funding transactions, to facilitate the early redemption of debt when cheaper or more suitable funding opportunities arise
- an understanding and awareness of financial risk (currency risk, interest rate risk and credit risk in particular)
- a willingness to exploit arbitrage opportunities in the financial markets, on a matched or unmatched basis.

Arbitrage is the process of buying or borrowing in one market, or segment of the market, and simultaneously selling or lending/investing in another market in order to guarantee a profit. Speculation, in contrast, involves entering transactions in the hope, but not the certainty, of making a profit.

When arbitrage is on a matched basis, the borrowing and investment, or the purchase and sale, have the same maturity or settlement date.

An example is the use of undrawn bank facilities or commercial paper facilities to borrow funds and then reinvest them at a profit on a matched basis. This is usually only possible by either investing in paper with a lower credit rating or by means of a tax-based arbitrage.

When arbitrage is on an unmatched basis, the terms of the borrowing and simultaneous reinvestment are different, and the loan and the investment will mature at different times.

Example 1
Alpha is a major company with an investment grade credit rating. It has a bank facility that enables it to borrow at LIBOR plus 50 basis points (0.50%). Three-month LIBOR is currently 6.5%. Omega, a company with a lower grade credit rating than Alpha, is issuing 90-day commercial paper on which the yield would be 7.2%.

Analysis
Alpha could draw on an unused part of its bank facility and borrow for three months (90 days) at 7% (6.5% + 50bp). It could use the funds to invest in Omega's commercial paper, to earn a profit of 0.2%.

However, Alpha's treasurer must be confident that the drawn funds for investing in Omega's paper will not be needed by the company for operational requirements during the next three months.

Example 2
Gamma is a large company with a high credit rating. It has a bank facility to borrow funds at LIBOR plus 50bp for up to 12 months. The yield curve is downward sloping at the moment, and LIBOR rates are as follows:

1 month	8.0%
2 months	7.8%
3 months	7.5%
6 months	7.3%

Delta, another public company with a similar credit rating to Gamma, has issued 3-month commercial paper yielding 8.0%.

Analysis
Suppose that the treasurer of Gamma takes the view that interest rates will come down eventually, but not as soon as the financial markets expect. An inverse yield curve is an indication that the markets expect interest rates to fall. Gamma could therefore arrange a borrowing and reinvesting transaction on a mismatched basis, and

- draw on its bank facility to borrow for six months at 7.8% (7.3% + 50bp)
- invest in Delta's CP at 8.0%.

Gamma would hope to reinvest the funds when Delta's CP matures at a rate higher than 7.8%, that should be possible if interest rates do not fall before then.

Gamma's treasurer also must be confident that the funds drawn to invest in Delta's CP will not be needed in the next six months. If Gamma needs the funds to meet an unexpected contingency, it might have to sell the CP in the secondary market at whatever price is available, to obtain the required funds.

Debt Management and the Yield Curve

Several key issues in debt profile management concern the yield curve, and the effect of possible changes in the yield curve on the optimal debt structure (debt profile) of a company.

A yield curve is a graph or table showing the current rate of interest on debt for a range of different terms to maturity. Maturities can range from one day (overnight) to 30 years (or even longer). The interest rate for each maturity is the fixed rate that would apply to new loans or issues of debt securities that are made now. The yield curve changes continually over time as interest rates alter.

A yield curve is constructed by selecting benchmark loans or issues of debt securities for different remaining terms to maturity, and taking the market interest rate on these debts as the current interest rate for that particular maturity. There is also a different yield curve for each currency. In the US, a yield curve can be constructed from the current market yields on selected issues of Treasury bills, Treasury notes and Treasury bonds. In the UK, for example, a yield curve is constructed from the London Interbank Offered Rate (LIBOR) for each of several different short-term maturities, and from the current redemption yields on selected government bond issues (gilts) for longer-term maturities.

Example

Selected US interest rates in July 1998 were as follows:

Treasury bills and bonds

Three-month	5.07	Three-year	5.46
Six-month	5.24	Five-year	5.46
One-year	5.35	10-year	5.45
Two-year	5.46	30-year	5.68

Analysis

The table in this example can be used to draw a graph (or bar chart) on how interest rates vary according to maturity. This is a yield curve up to a ten-year maturity.

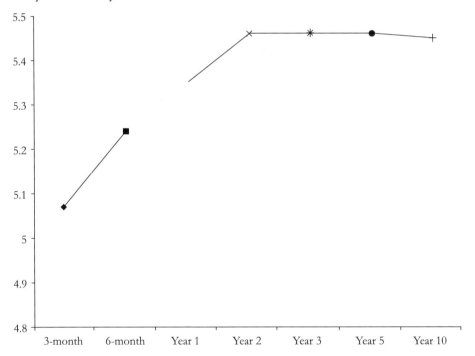

It is important to understand what a yield curve shows. Two particular factors are significant.

- The yield curve indicates what a borrower might have to pay to borrow now, for a given term-to-maturity, if the borrowing is arranged at a fixed rate of interest.

● The yield curve shows current interest rates. Because interest rates change, the yield curve can be expected to change in the future.

Market rates of interest change continually, usually by small amounts from day to day, but sometimes by large amounts over time.

When interest rates change, there could be a general rise or fall, so that rates for all maturities go up or down. Also there could be a change in the cost of borrowing for one term relative to the cost of borrowing for a shorter or longer term. For example, the cost of a 12-month loan could go up from 7% to 7.5%, while the cost of a five-year loan remains unchanged at 8% or falls to 7.7%, or goes up but by a smaller amount from 8% to 8.25%.

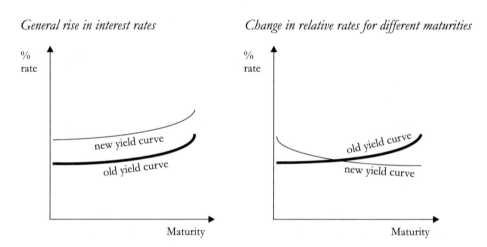

General rise in interest rates   *Change in relative rates for different maturities*

Yield Curve and Borrowing Costs

The interest rates in a yield curve are not necessarily the rates at which a company could borrow, but the yield curve is nevertheless a useful indicator of interest rates for different maturities. For example, in the UK, the yield curve for short maturities is the current London Interbank Offered Rate. A company might be able to borrow at LIBOR + 1%, for any maturity up to 12 months. The yield curve, showing the LIBOR rate for different maturities, would identify which term of borrowing up to 12 months is currently the cheapest.

Shape of the Yield Curve

The level of short-term interest rates often can be much lower or much higher than interest rates for longer maturities.

There are three main yield curve shapes:

- positive or classical (upward sloping)
- negative or inverse (downward sloping)
- flat.

There are several major influences on the shape of the yield curve. Interest rates for long maturities are higher or lower than interest rates for shorter maturities according to which of these influences happens to be greater at the time. The main influences are

- demand and supply in the debt markets (the deployment of cash)
- market expectations of future interest rate movements that are in turn affected mainly by expectations of future changes in the rate of inflation
- government policy. A government can, intentionally or otherwise, influence interest rates through its dealings in the money markets or bond markets.

Yield Curves

The yield curve can move up or down over time as interest rates for all maturities rise or fall, while leaving the basic shape of the yield curve unaltered. It can also change shape as the relative levels of short-term and longer-term interest rates change.

A yield curve is normally upward sloping, or positive that means that long-term yields (bond yields) are commonly higher than short-term yields (money-market yields).

Progressively higher yields as the tenure of the loan increases reflect

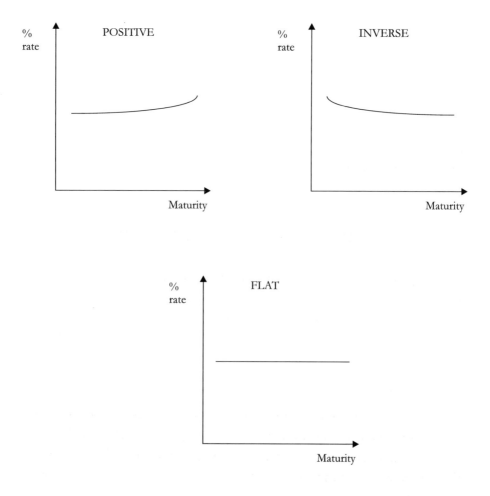

- the higher compensation demanded by lenders for the risk of committing funds for a longer period, and
- the higher cost conceded by borrowers for the comfort of securing fixed-rate funding for a longer period, and therefore reducing risk and uncertainty in the future costs and availability of borrowing.

In the absence of significant swings in the rate of inflation, a positive yield curve will apply.

A mildly positive yield curve is the sign of an economy in equilibrium with an outlook for a low and stable rate of return. It is no coincidence that the German, Swiss and Japanese yield curves have adopted this shape for much of the past decade, although recent problems in the German and Japanese economies have been unsettling for interest rates.

A negative yield curve indicates expectations of a large fall in the rate of inflation in the foreseeable future. This is because the expected fall in nominal interest rates must be large enough to offset the normal requirement of lenders for a higher yield on longer-term lending – implicit in a classical positive yield curve.

Yield Curve Opportunities

The shape of a yield curve can be crucial to debt management because it dictates the cost of funding for any given maturity (term of borrowing). Periodically opportunities can arise, from the current shape of the yield curve, to reduce the cost of funding a business with little attached risk.

Negative Yield Curve Opportunities

When the yield curve is negative, because the market expects the rate of inflation to fall, opportunities can arise for a company to borrow long term and reinvest short term at a profit. The risk will be limited, provided the company knows that eventually it will need the long-term funds for its own use, and is simply borrowing them earlier than necessary.

Example
Gamma, a multinational company with a high credit rating, needs to borrow $50 million in one year's time for a nine-year term. It will borrow at a fixed rate, either by issuing fixed-rate bonds or by borrowing at a variable rate and arranging an interest-rate swap to convert the variable rate obligations to fixed-rate payments. Gamma's chief operating officer has noticed that the yield curve is steeply negative, and the company could

- borrow now for ten years at a fixed rate of 7%, and
- invest the funds for one year to earn 9%.

Analysis

The company can arrange its nine-year funding from years one to ten by borrowing now for ten years and investing the money for the first year, at a profit of $1 million ($50 million x (9% – 7%)). Taking the reinvestment profit as a reduction in net interest costs, the effect of this would be to reduce the overall cost of borrowing the $50 million from 7% to about 6% per annum. (The workings are not shown.)

However, there is some risk with a policy of committing the company to a ten-year borrowing a year earlier than required. Interest rates during the subsequent year could fall below 6%, and Gamma will have lost the opportunity to borrow at this low rate, having already locked in the funding cost with the ten-year borrowing. The negative yield curve indicates expectations of a fall in short-term rates, but not necessarily a corresponding fall in long-term rates, certainly not a fall to a nine-year rate of 6% or less in one year's time.

A further benefit of this kind of transaction is to lock in the cost of funding and remove the risk of long-term interest rates rising, involving Gamma in a higher cost of borrowing in one year's time. However, a negative yield curve indicates that such an outcome is unlikely.

A corporate borrower can benefit from this type of interest rate play at little risk. This could be a reason for heavy borrowing activity in a long-dated bond market. If the yield curve were negative, companies can make bond issues ahead of their funding requirement to take advantage of the yield curve opportunities.

Positive Yield Curve Opportunities

When the yield curve is positive, companies usually cannot benefit (with little risk) from the differences between shorter-term and longer-term interest rates. To profit from an upward-sloping yield curve, a company could borrow short term at a fixed rate and reinvest (also at a fixed rate) for a longer term. There are serious risks with this strategy, however, because a company that borrows short term and reinvests for a longer term must negotiate new finance when the short-term loan matures. For example, suppose that a company borrows for one year at 6% and reinvests for five years at a fixed rate of 7%. The one-year loan will have to be replaced or renewed at the end of one year. The risks facing the company would be that

- the general level of interest rates could rise by the time the maturing short-term loan has to be renewed or replacement finance obtained (in the example above, borrowing rates could rise above 7%); and

the company might be unable to obtain new finance when the short-term loan matures. It might even be unable to repay the one-year loan. This risk of not being able to obtain replacement finance is known as refinancing risk.

Refinancing

Every company that borrows funds, whether occasionally or regularly, must either repay the debt out of operational cash flows, or obtain new finance to replace the debt at maturity.

Refinancing is a process of obtaining new funds to replace debts that are due (or overdue) for repayment. There are various methods of refinancing, for example:

- renewing a committed bank facility when the facility expires
- obtaining new bank loans to redeem maturing loans
- issuing bonds and using the proceeds to redeem maturing loans
- issuing equity and using the proceeds to repay debt (loans or debt securities, such as bonds or commercial paper).

Refinancing can often be achieved with little difficulty, particularly when the company has low gearing and a good credit rating. Occasionally, however, the problems associated with refinancing can be quite severe, particularly when

- banks are reluctant to lend to companies, particularly high-geared companies (except perhaps at high rates of interest), and
- a company with a large burden of maturing debts suffers a downturn in profits, so that its profits are barely adequate to cover interest costs. Banks could refuse new refinancing loans to a struggling company.

In some cases, particularly during an economic recession, a company's profits and cash flows might slump to a level where it is unable to meet current interest payments on its debts and will clearly be unable to repay existing debts at maturity. When a company fails to make a payment of interest or debt principal on schedule, and is therefore in default on one or more loans, it will be forced to ask its creditors for emergency refinancing. More usually, a company breaches a loan covenant, e.g. an interest cover covenant or a minimum gearing covenant, and the event of default leads to refinancing discussions with the lending banks, or the trustees for the bondholders, etc.. In effect, companies in default fall into the hands of their lending banks that can decide

- whether or not to provide sufficient funds to keep the company in business, and
- how the company's affairs should be managed until a refinancing package is agreed.

The banks will also be in a powerful bargaining position during the financing negotiations with the company.

Interim Refinancing

Opportunities can arise during the life of a loan to refinance on more favorable terms. This can occur, for example, when thc borrower's creditworthiness has improved since the original loan was arranged. If the improvement is substantial, the company might be able repay the original loan and at the same time negotiate a replacement loan at a new lower rate. The money from the new loan would be used to repay the current loan.

Mending the Balance Sheet

The history of corporate financing in the US since the 1980s provides some interesting lessons about the choice of a debt-equity mix. In the 1980s, there were numerous leveraged buyouts (many arranged by Kohlberg Kravis Roberts) in which companies were purchased mainly with borrowings. When in 1989 the recession hit the US, many such companies found that their debt burden was too high, and interest charges were jeopardizing profits.

From 1989 onwards, some of these companies sought to alter their debt-equity mix by raising new equity capital in order to pay off some debt. This arrangement has been called a distressed exchange offer or mending the balance sheet. Two examples in 1991 (both KKR-arranged leveraged buyouts in the 1980s) were RJR Nabisco, the tobacco and consumer products firm, and Duracell, the batteries group. As a consequence, in each of these cases, the company's equity capital was increased and its debt capital reduced.

When new equity issues are made to mend the balance sheet and replace debt with equity, operating profits should cover the cost of interest on the remaining debt. As a result, the company should be able to meet its debt payment obligations and earn profits (and dividends) for stockholders.

If an equity issue is not big enough, the interest cost of the remaining debt might still be too high for the company's operating profits. In such a case the issue would not then be a long-term solution to the company's financial problems.

Example 1
In January 1998 Eurotunnel that runs the tunnel beneath the English Channel, announced negotiations with its lender banks for a further reorganization of its £7.8 billion junior debt. The debt had already been rescheduled in 1995, and after two years of negotiations the creditor banks had finally unanimously approved the plan in November 1997, averting the threat of receivership. The restructuring followed a decrease in revenue by 20% following a fire in the tunnel and a loss in 1997 of £611 million (1996: £685 million), after net financing costs of £633 million (1996: £615 million).

The plan resulted in Eurotunnel (through its UK arm, Eurotunnel PLC, or EPLC and its French arm, Eurotunnel SA, or ESA) giving the banks 769 million new stocks amounting to 45.5% of its equity, in return for a write-off of £1 billion in debt. The banks also received warrants and other securities paying lower long-term interest, reducing the company's annual interest bill by approximately 40% per annum.

Details of the restructuring were as follows:

- £908 million of the existing junior debt was replaced by the issue of 769,230,800 new units to the banks, at an issue price of £0.59. In addition, FFr5.84 new units were offered to unitholders
- £906 million of the junior debt was converted into 645,161,300 equity notes, issued at par to the banks. Each note consisted of one French franc note and one sterling note
- £1,092 million of the junior debt was converted into Participating Loan Notes, issued at par to the creditor banks. These consisted of two series of twinned notes, one sterling-denominated and one franc-denominated
- An equivalent of £1,366 million of the junior debt was exchanged for a Resettable Facility within a Revised Credit Agreement. The facility comprised a French franc tranche of FFr7,336 million and a sterling tranche of £624 million
- The balance of the junior debt (£3,516 million) was to remain as residual junior debt
- A bonus issue of 2003 and 2001 warrants was made to qualifying unitholders. Three 2003 warrants, or eight 2001 warrants, entitled a holder to subscribe on exercise for one EPLC ordinary stock and one ESA ordinary stock, issued in the form of units. The warrants were issued to unitholders on the basis of one 2001 and one 2003 warrant for every unit held.

There have been many other cases, however, where successful mending of the balance sheet has occurred.

Example 2

In September 1991, British Aerospace plc announced a two for five rights issue to raise about £432 million. The company was expanding and had a major program of new investment, but at the same time site closures in parts of its business were incurring large rationalization costs. Most of the group's non-defense operations were facing near term pressures on both profitability and cash flow. As a consequence, the company's management, having reviewed funding requirements, decided that the equity base of the company should be expanded, and the net proceeds of the issue applied to the reduction of the group's borrowings.

When the issue was announced, the company's debts were about £2 billion and its stockholders' funds about £2.5 billion. leverage was therefore quite high, and losses threatened to make the financial position worse.

Analysis
The rights issue was underwritten; therefore the company successfully raised the funds it was seeking. Investor support was disappointing, however, and a large proportion of the new stocks was left with the underwriters. At the time investors were not convinced by the company's economic arguments and strategy for recovery. The stock price fell sharply. At the time of the rights issue, the stock price had fallen to around the issue price (380p) and subsequently fell much further (below 110p) before eventually recovering strongly, increasing to over 580p by mid-1998.

Nevertheless, the company successfully achieved both its immediate objective of raising new equity and reducing its debt burden, as well as its longer-term objective of achieving recovery in its businesses.

Forced Refinancing

If an actual or potential breach of a loan covenant forces a company to negotiate a refinancing package with its bank(s), the company will have a very weak negotiating position. However, if the company owes the banks it is often in their interest to assist the company to trade out of trouble, thereby improving the prospects for eventual payment of the debts. Even so, the process of refinancing can be a tremendous burden on a company and its management. The company, in effect, has to face up to the consequences of wrongly managing its capital structure, and borrowing in excess of its ability to repay.

Banks normally will seek several concessions from a company in a rescue refinancing negotiation:

- substantial front-end fees that are typically between 1% and 5% of the value of the refinancing loans
- higher interest rates (i.e. a higher margin over LIBOR for facilities and term loans). It is not uncommon for new loans to be arranged with margins of about 3% to 5% higher than on the old loans
- security for the new loans
- a detailed business plan showing how the company can expect to trade out of trouble, whether by asset sales, or by cutting costs
- in many cases, a change of management
- monthly or quarterly testing arrangements, to monitor the company's progress.

If the banks believe that the company can survive and improve its profits and cash flows, they will agree to provide new capital and reschedule the existing debts. New loan covenants will be agreed, based on the business plan projections, so that there should not be an event of default on the loans provided the planning targets are met. The revised covenants will be set at a level close to planned performance levels, to keep pressure on management to achieve the required results.

The banks will also make it clear to management that until the loans are repaid the company is being run for the banks' benefit. Therefore management will be restricted in the major business decisions they can take until the crisis has passed and the company's debts have been repaid.

In some countries, such as Germany and Japan, generally banks have supported companies in financial difficulties. Banks, however, can afford to support companies only if their own financial position remains strong.

Committee of Banks

In some cases of enforced refinancing, a company will have outstanding debts to a large number of banks. With cross-default clauses in many loan covenants, the company will be required to agree a refinancing package with all of them. To simplify the negotiating process, a committee of banks will be set up to enter discussions with the company on behalf of all the banks. The committee usually will consist of representatives from the banks that are owed the most. Because the committee cannot reach an agreement without first obtaining consent to the package from all the banks, negotiations can be very lengthy, sometimes lasting several months. Typically, some banks will agree to provide further interim finance to the company during the negotiating process, to keep the company afloat until a refinancing package is agreed and in place.

After agreeing a package, the committee of banks will also expect to monitor the progress of the company, to make sure that its agreements are being upheld, e.g. that loan covenants are not breached, and that the company sells off assets on schedule, if it has promised asset sales to raise money for repaying loans.

New Finance or Rescheduling Loans?

Refinancing packages vary in character. Sometimes, the company needs little more than a renewal of existing loans, i.e. a deferral of redemption dates. In other situations, a company also will need some new loans to raise extra capital. Very occasionally, banks might agree to exchange equity for debts, i.e. to accept stocks in the company as payment for some of the company's debts.

News Corporation

The case of News Corporation, the multinational media group that negotiated a widely reported refinancing package in 1990-91, highlights several features of such deals.

At the time of the renegotiations, Rupert Murdoch, head of News Corporation, admitted that the company probably had too much short-term debt in its capital structure, and the balance of borrowing had therefore probably been wrong. The company had borrowed much of its debt short term from the late 1980s, because short-term funds were much cheaper at the time. Although there was a need for longer-term debt, the company delayed long-term borrowing decisions, expecting interest rates to fall.

Problems began to emerge in 1990 when a number of Japanese banks withdrew from the Australian money markets where News Corp had a A$200 million commercial paper program, and would regularly borrow funds overnight, or for seven days or 30 days. The withdrawal of the Japanese banks meant the loss of key investors in News Corp's paper, and a regular supply of short-term funding virtually disappeared.

Sale and leaseback arrangements, another regular source of funds for the company, also became much more difficult. Banks were becoming reluctant to agree deals except at very high interest rates.

In addition, the company had about $2.9 billion of debt scheduled to mature between September 1990 and June 1991. In September, borrowings of $500 million were rolled over for a further period, but with some difficulty, and News Corp's financial problem was becoming apparent.

Negotiations began with the company's banks. Management was surprised to find that the company owed money to about 150 banks, some original lenders had transferred loans to other banks. The main lending banks at the time (Citibank, Midland, Lloyds, Deutsche Bank, Crédit Lyonnais, Manufacturers Hanover, Security Pacific, Commonwealth Bank of Australia, Westpac) had to be identified, and the full extent and nature of the company's debts established. The banks wanted assurance that the company's net assets exceeded the total amount of its debts.

Due to the complexity of the many loans and guarantees, a committee of banks that was set up to consider News Corp's position decided that a financial restructuring was not possible, i.e. replacing old loans with new ones, and with fewer lending banks. Instead, it was decided that the company's existing loans should be extended, with every bank locked in and treated equally. News Corp asked for loan extensions of about five or seven years, but an extension of just three years was finally agreed.

During the negotiation process, News Corp was granted a credit line from the banks to keep it going. Negotiations lasted several months, and some loans reached maturity during that time. These were rolled up until the deal was completed. An increasing percentage of News Corp's debts were becoming short term, increasing the risk of a lender calling the company in default on its repayment obligations, and so initiating legal action.

The terms of the $8.2 billion refinancing deal were agreed early in 1991.

- About $7.6 billion of existing debt was restructured over three years, to be repaid by February 1994. The company had to pay an extra margin of 1% (100 basis points) on existing facilities and a 1% up-front arrangement fee.
- A further one-year credit of US$600 million was obtained from a group of banks, at an interest rate on average of 21/4% over money market rates.
- There would be a success fee of 1% on any outstanding debt after three years.

The company agreed to reduce its total debts by about $800 million after 12 months, and a further $400 million in the next year or so. It was understood that the company would sell off some of its assets to achieve this aim.

While the agreement was in effect, the company's dividend was restricted to no more than A$0.10 each year, and the Murdoch family interests agreed to take dividends in stocks rather than cash. The company also agreed to quarterly meetings with a committee of its bankers to discuss progress, i.e. results and operations of the company, with the aim of ensuring that the company would keep to its debt repayment schedule and stick to its loan covenants. The main covenants were to maintain a minimum ratio of interest to operating cash flow and a minimum ratio of operating earnings to debt.

Since the refinancing of News Corp was agreed in 1991, the company has enjoyed a period of strong trading performance, justifying the decision of the banks to support the refinancing agreement.

Summary

Refinancing can be either

- opportunistic, i.e. a company can take advantage of current conditions to improve its capital structure or debt costs, or
- enforced, i.e. a company is forced to renegotiate its debts with its banks because of an actual or expected breach of covenants.

When enforced refinancing takes place, a company's management has temporarily lost control of their financing arrangements and is dependent on the banks. Until the loans are successfully repaid, a company must comply with its banks' requirements as to capital structuring and operating activities.

Glossary

Amortization of Debt
Schedule for the repayment of loan principal.

Beta
A factor (in the capital-asset pricing model) that measures the volatility of returns on a share against average stock market returns.

Capital-Asset Pricing Model (CAPM)
A mathematical model that can be used to measure the cost of equity in individually (quoted) companies.

Cost of Capital
The return required by providers of capital; therefore the cost of finance for a company.

Covenant
Undertaking by a borrower to its lenders, as part of the loan agreement. A breach of covenant is an act of default, giving the lender the right to take action (if required) for the recovery of the debt.

Credit Rating
Measurement of the creditworthiness of an organization with respect to loan stock it has issued. Large bond or loan issues are often given credit ratings by specialist agencies – the highest credit rating is AAA (triple-A).

Debt Maturity Profile
Pattern of maturity dates for outstanding debts and bank facilities.

Deferred Equity
An instrument that is not yet in the form of equity shares, but could at sometime be used to subscribe for new equity shares (e.g. convertibles, share options, share warrants).

Dividend Growth Model
A mathematical model that can be used to estimate the fair value of a share, given assumptions about future dividend growth and the cost of equity capital. The share price is the present value of expected future dividends, discounted at the cost of equity.

Earnings Dilution
Fall in earnings per share.

Eurobonds
Long-term debt securities issued in the international bond markets. They provide a method of borrowing directly from investors rather than banks.

Eurocurrency
Currency deposited with and lent by banks outside the currency's country of origin.

Facility
Arrangement with a bank for borrowing funds as and when required, up to the limit of the facility.

Fixed Costs
Costs that remain at a fixed level, regardless of any increase or decrease in operational activity.

Fixed Rate
An interest rate that is set at the start of a transaction (e.g. loan) and does not vary during the term of the transaction.

Floating Rate (Variable Rate)
An interest rate that is reset at predetermined intervals (reset dates or rollover dates) during the life of a transaction, e.g. a loan.

Hybrid Instruments
These are financial instruments that have some of the characteristics of equity and some of the characteristics of debt; neither straight equity nor straight debt.

Junk Bonds
Unsecured non-investment grade bonds, yielding a comparatively high rate of interest. Bonds with a credit rating Ba1/BB+ and below fall into this category. There is an active junk bond market.

Leverage
The term normally refers to financial leverage that is the proportion of debt capital relative to equity in a company's capital structure. High leverage means a high debt:equity ratio. Operational leverage refers to the relative proportion of fixed costs to variable costs in the cost structure of a business. High leverage occurs when fixed costs are high relative to variable costs.

LIBOR
London Interbank Offered Rate. Interest rate at which creditworthy banks lend to each other short term (in the money markets).

Mending the Balance Sheet
Issuing equity and using the money raised from the issue to pay off outstanding debts.

Offshore Financial Center
Finance subsidiary established in another country where tax regulations are less onerous, e.g. a tax haven.

Operational Cash Flow
The net cash flow from business operations. As a rough guide, operational cash flow can be estimated as profit before tax plus depreciation charges (a non-cash charge against profits).

EBIT
Earnings before interest and tax.

Refinancing
The process of obtaining new funds to replace debts that are due or overdue for payment. Refinancings can be either planned/orderly or forced. Companies that are in breach of loan covenants could be forced to seek refinancing.

Rescue Rights
Rights issue of new shares, this is where the money is used to provide the company with urgently needed finance, e.g. to mend the balance sheet.

Stock Market Rating
A stock's market price relative to earnings per share, as compared with stocks of other stock market companies.

Treasury Bill
A US government short-term security sold to the public each week, maturing between 91 and 182 days.

Variable Costs
Costs that rise as operational activity increases and fall as operational activity decreases.

Yield Curve

A term used to describe how current interest rates vary according to the term-to-maturity of the loan or deposit. When longer-term interest rates are higher than shorter-term rates, the yield curve is upward sloping or normal (positive). When longer-term interest rates are lower than shorter-term rates, the yield curve is inverse (negative). These interest rate comparisons can be shown on a graph; hence the term yield curve.

Index

Acquisitions 60
Actual cash flows 18
Actual profits 28
All-equity companies 53
Alternative Investment
Market (AIM) 27
Amortization 64, 66
Amortized repayment 70
Annual returns 29
Arbitrage 108
Asset backing 41
Asset disposals 49
Assets, core 19
Assets, fixed 14

Bank facilities 64, 71
Bank lines 18
Bank loans 120
Beta factors 32, 33
Bloombergs 34
Bond issues 46, 70
Bond market 64, 66
Bond yields 113
Bondholders 45
Bonds 47
Bonds, fixed-rate 82
Bonds, government 66
Bonds, money-markets 113
Book leverage 38
Borrowing 12
Borrowing costs 78, 112
Borrowing terms 115
Borrowing, fixed-rate 14
Borrowing, variable 14
Bulk payments 19
Bullet repayment 66

Business cycles 43

Capital cost 26
Capital debt 34
Capital gains 27, 86
Capital investment 45
Capital losses 27
Capital markets 73, 64, 108
Capital requirements 101
Capital structure
planning 52
Capital structuring 16
Capital, debt 27, 34, 35, 64,
86, 92
Capital, equity 34, 86, 122
Capital-asset pricing model
(CAPM) 28, 30, 31
Cash cows 52
Cash flow 26, 37
Cash flow forecast 12
Cash flows 120
Cash management 15
Cash requirements 66
Cash surplus 16
Commercial paper 47,
77, 108
Commercial risks 43
Commitment fee 71
Contingency funding 12
Contingency requirements
18, 20, 71
Convertible bonds 47, 82
Convertible preferred stocks
82, 84
Convertibles 86
Core assets 19

Core funding 18
Core funding
requirements 18
Core profitability 39
Cost of equity 27
Costs, fixed 44
Costs, variable 44
Covenant, interest cover 121
Covenant, loan 124
Covenant, minimum
gearing 121
Covenants 42, 64, 76
Covenants, revised 125
Credit rating 53, 77, 78
Credit risk 78
Cross-border currency
flows 69
Cross-border transactions 61
Cross-default clauses 125
Currency swaps market 69
Currency swaps 64

Debt 26, 63-80
Debt capital 27, 28, 35, 49,
64, 92
Debt finance 48, 64
Debt fluctuation 71
Debt funding 34, 36, 65,
Debt instruments 71
Debt management 15 108,
110, 115
Debt markets 41
Debt maturity profile 104
Debt payment
obligations 122
Debt portfolio 104

Debt principal 28
Debt profile 64, 104, 105
Debt profile
  management 103-118
Debt securities 64, 77, 110
Debt, capital 34
Debt, equity 19
Debt, fixed-rate 68
Debt, floating-rate 68
Debt, long-term 18, 19, 46
Debt, rated 77
Debt, unrated 77
Debt-equity mix 121
Defensive stocks 32
Deferral of redemption 126
Deferred equity 87
Development strategy 101
Distressed exchange
  offer 122
Distributable reserves 55
Dividend cover 52
Dividend cuts 62
Dividend payments 14, 27
Dividend policy 55, 62
Dividend receipts 14
Dividends 27

Earnings dilution 48, 54
Economic cycle 33
Emergency refinancing 120
End date 14
Enforced refinancing 125
Equity 12, 26, 28, 51-62
Equity capital 29, 34, 45,
  53, 122
Equity debt 19
Equity dividends 87
Equity finance 39
Equity funding 18, 34, 64
Equity instruments 71
Equity investors 101
Equity issues 48, 7
Equity stockholders 45
Equity stocks 27
Equity warrant bonds 84, 86
Equity warrants 82
Equity, deferred 87
Eurobonds 48
Eurocommercial paper 77

Euromarkets 48
Europaper 86
Exchange rates 69
Exchangeable stocks 85
Exercise price 84
External funds 11-24

Finance, equity 39
Financial instruments 26,
  81-90, 92
Financial planners 18
Financial risk 43, 44,
  98, 108
Fixed assets 14
Fixed costs 44
Fixed dividends 87
Fixed rate bonds 82
Fixed-rate borrowing 14
Fixed-rate debt 68
Fixed-rate loan 34
Fixed-rate obligation 68
Floating rate debt 68
Floating-rate obligation 68
Forced refinancing 124
Forecasting error 18
Front-end fees 125
Funding options 25-50
Funding policy 21
Funding pool 66
Funding requirements
  18, 101
Funding sources 64
Funding surpluses 22, 93
Funding, core 18
Funding, core, long-term 19
Funding, core, short-term 18
Funding, debt 34, 36, 65, 70
Funding, equity 18, 34
Funding, long-term 18, 71
Funding, matched 65
Funding, short-term 18
Funding, unmatched 65
Future growth 29

Gearing ratio 76
Gilts 110
Gordon dividend growth
  model 28
Government bond issues 110

Government bonds 30, 66
Government intervention 43

Hedging loans 70
Home starts 45
Hybrid instruments 71

Individual stocks 30
Inflation 29
Initial public
  offering (IPO) 57
Institutional investors 58
Instruments, debt 71
Instruments, equity 71
Instruments, hybrid 71
Interest cover covenant 121
Interest payments 14, 28
Interest rate basis 64
Interest rate swaps 68
Interest receipts 14
Interim finance 126
Interim refinancing 121
Investment, risk-free 30
Investors 26, 54
Issue, equity 77
Issue, rights 57, 58
Issues, bond 46, 120
Issues, equity 48, 120
Issues, government
  bonds 110
Issues, stock 46

Junior debt 122, 123

Leverage 26, 39, 41, 42, 43
Leverage level 100
Leverage risk 98
Leverage target 100
LIBOR 34, 36, 67, 109,
  110, 112
Loan covenant 42, 48,
  49, 124
Loan creditors 99
Loan markets 108
Loan providers 41
London Business School 34
Long-term debt 18, 19, 46
Long-term funding 12, 14,
  18, 70

Losses 45

Market debt instrument 35
Market conditions 47
Market recession 20
Market risk 31
Matched funding 65
Maturity period 64
Maturity profile 93
Medium-term notes 48
Minimum gearing
  covenant 121
Money markets 108
Money-market bonds 113
Moody's 79
Multiple Option Facility
(MOF) 72

NASDAQ 27
Negative cash flows 16
Net income 44
New capital 45
New debt 36
Nil-tax regimes 75
Non-equity stocks 83
Non-resident companies 75
Notes 47
Notes, medium-term 48

Offshore financial centers 74
Operating income 44
Operational leverage 43
Operational profit 26

Payment schedule 37
Payments, dividend 14
Payments, interest 14
Placing of issues 57, 58, 64
Planning horizon 14
Pre-emption rights 58, 59
Preferred stock 47, 83, 87
Price sensitivity 43
Product obsolescence 43
Profit margins 52
Profit ratios 52
Promissory notes,
  short-term 35
Public spending 45

Quantitative accuracy 12

Raising capital 12
Rated debt 77
Rating agencies 77
Receipts, dividend 14
Receipts, interest 14
Redeeming loans 120
Refinancing 104, 119-130
Refinancing loans 125
Refinancing risk 65
Retained earnings 62, 96
Reuters 34
Revised covenants 125
Rights issue 57, 58
Risk factor 28
Risk-free investment 30
Risks, commercial 43

Scrip dividends 57
Secondary markets 73
Sensitivity analysis 12
Short-term cyclical
  funding 18
Short-term funding 12, 18
Short-term promissory
  notes 35
Standard and Poor's 79
Standard covenant 38
Stock capital 42
Stock issues 46
Stock market analysis 37
Stock market rating 26, 37
Stock market valuation 43
Stock option schemes 57, 59
Stock price 27
Stock price falls 27
Stock rating 54
Stock reserves 42
Stock-for-stock offers 61
Stockholders 54
Stocks 60
Stocks, preferred 47
Strategic plan 189
Sustainable profit 39
Swaps, currency 64
Syndicated bank loans 48

Tax considerations 74
Tax havens 74
Tax relief 38
Tax treatment 70
Tax-based arbitrage 108
Term loan 64
Timing accuracy 13
Treasury bills 110
Treasury bonds 110
Treasury department 29
Treasury notes 110

Unmatched funding 65
Unrated debt 77
Unsystematic risk 31
Unutilized funds 105
US commercial paper
  market 77
Utilized funds 105

Variable costs 44
Variable-rate borrowing 14
Variable-rate loan 34
Volatile profits 38

WACD 35, 36
Window markets 74
Worse-case scenario 20

Yield 29
Yield curve 68, 10, 112, 113
Yields, bonds 113

Zero-coupon convertibles 83